Retreat Leader Guide

WORKBOOK

RICHARD T. CASE

Dedication / Acknowledgements

I wish to dedicate this course to and thank my wife, Linda, and our ministry leaders who received this important aspect of God's life for all His children. We were together at a leader retreat in France when we worked through this material. We understood that deliverance and overcoming is not an event, but learning to process our adversities, difficulties and strained relationships through to receiving the life of God that provides the power to overcome and then remain delivered. David's life provides so many wonderful examples of how God worked in his life through all his interesting circumstances that we all can relate to. There is no system and not one way to experience this—rather truths that are to be applied personally in unique circumstances. Since this time in France, we all have been delivered and have overcome hardships such that we now know that no matter what the world throws at us, we will have victory. And, it is a privilege to experience this as a married couple and as a member of a faithful community that walks together through this. We now can teach and encourage others in the same truths that will provide the hope that we all need to continue to deal with life difficulties. Thank you, Linda and ministry team.

These leaders are:
Jake & Mary Beckel
Joe & Leigh Bogar
Heath & Rebecca Cardie
Rich & Janet Cocchiaro
Larry & Sherry Collett
Scott & Kristen Cornell
David & Melissa Dunkel
Tom & Susanne Ewing
Rick & Kelly Ferris
Joel & Christina Gunn
Scott & Terry Hitchcock
Rick & Nancy Hoover
Tad & Monica Jones
Ed & Becky Kobel
Don & Rachelle Light
Chris and Heidi May
Terry & Josephine Noetzel
Towanda Norton
Steve & Carolyn Van Ooteghem
Preston & Lynda Pitts
Dan & Kathy Rocconi
Bob & Keri Rockwell
John & Michelle Santaferraro
Allyson & Denny Weinberg
Neal & Kathy Weisenburger

OVERCOMING & DELIVERANCE – STUDY OF THE LIFE OF DAVID
PUBLISHED BY LIVING WATERS—ABIDE MINISTRIES
7615 Lemon Gulch Way
Castle Rock, CO 80108

ISBN: 979-8-218-13694-9

Publisher's Cataloging-in-Publication data

Names:
Title:
Description: .
Identifiers: ISBN | LCCN
Subjects:

Printed in the United States of America 2024 — 2nd ed

TABLE OF CONTENTS

LESSON 1: THE CONDITION OF THE WORLD & WHY WE ALL WILL EXPERIENCE DIFFICULTIES; AND WHAT THEN DOES GOD PROMISE TO OVERCOME THE WORLD?

Welcome to our course, *Overcoming and Deliverance: A Study of the Life of David.* We will use the life of David as an example of scriptural truth of how we overcome and are delivered from circumstantial and soul issues/wounds in our lives. We have issues in life. We have things that come against us, things that are difficult, circumstances that are beyond our ability to resolve, wounds that we carry that oppress the ability to have freedom. God says, *I've overcome it all—let Me guide you to join Me in that overcoming.* Deliverance is about our soul, heart issues. We have woundedness. We have patterns. We have things in which we would like to improve. We will study this in depth so that we have a better understanding of whether or not a simple prayer gives us permanent freedom or resolution of our issues. It's not just an experience in one particular moment, but we will learn to experience true overcoming and true deliverance.

What does Jesus say about what we will experience in this world? Why is this important to understand? What is the good news about the remedy for the problem? Why is that important to believe?

> "God wants to bless you with things of the world—not for you to chase them, as that is self-centered, but rather to enjoy them as given by God."

Read John 16:33:

³³ I have said these things to you, that in me you may have peace. In the world you will have tribulation. But take heart; I have overcome the world."

____

____

____

____

____

____

____

LESSON 1: THE CONDITION OF THE WORLD & WHY WE ALL WILL EXPERIENCE DIFFICULTIES; AND WHAT THEN DOES GOD PROMISE TO OVERCOME THE WORLD?

In the world, you're going to have tribulation—trouble, stress, difficulty, pressure. What exactly is the world? It's not the actual stuff of the world. God says as part of life, you have to receive, use, and enjoy the stuff of the world—such as houses, automobiles, clothes, etc.—but that is not the world itself. The world, as defined here, is the selfishness and the system of selfishness—along with the work of the enemy that comes against the will of God. God wants to bless you with things of the world—not for you to chase them, as that is self-centered, but rather to enjoy them as given by God. So, it's really the self-centered system and the influence of the enemy in a very difficult, frustrating place—here in the physical— because we have entropy, which is everything on this Earth is going to kill, steal, and destroy.

If you look at that definition, why does it have to be overcome? Two reasons:

1. The world is not of God, and the results of living in the world are trouble and difficulty.

2. As we try to resolve the trouble of the world on our won, we do not overcome it, and it tends to get worse.

Left alone, what are you going to experience? The destruction of things, the opposition of things, the heaviness of things, the tribulation of things. Jesus said, *In the world, you're going to have trouble, but don't fret.* He says He's done what? He's overcome it.

What does *overcome* mean? It means to triumph over it. It still exists, but it doesn't bother you. It doesn't hold power over you, and since God has overcome it, He will restore this issue back to wholeness—back into harmony. God says that we are living in a destructive place. We are living in a world of trouble, that includes our soul wounds. We need deliverance from our soul issues and the circumstances that are coming against us. He has overcome all that. The circumstances that exist in your life, do not prevent Him from restoring to you the beautiful things of life if you allow Him. Let Him transform you—not manage the soul issues but restore back to you the fullness of His abundant life for you.

Will this restore us back to where Adam and Eve were? No. How come? They lived in a perfect world. They had no soul issues. They had no circumstances that were subject to the destruction of the enemy. When they failed to follow God and handed over authority to the enemy, we were all sentenced to live in a sinful world—a world of kill, steal, and destroy. Our nature is a sin nature, a self-centered nature, so our situation and our nature are not permanently brought back to that of Adam and Eve, but we can still have restoration and deliverance.

LESSON 1: THE CONDITION OF THE WORLD & WHY WE ALL WILL EXPERIENCE DIFFICULTIES; AND WHAT THEN DOES GOD PROMISE TO OVERCOME THE WORLD?

Knowing that we can overcome the trouble that we will experience in the world, what specific trouble will we be able to overcome, and what does Christ promise us about this? What is important for how we approach these issues?

Read Isaiah 61:1–4:

The Year of the LORD'S Favor

61 The Spirit of the LORD GOD is upon me,
   because the LORD has anointed me
to bring good news to the poor;[a]
   he has sent me to bind up the brokenhearted,
to proclaim liberty to the captives,
   and the opening of the prison to those who are bound;[b]
² to proclaim the year of the LORD'S favor,
   and the day of vengeance of our God;
   to comfort all who mourn;
³ to grant to those who mourn in Zion—
   to give them a beautiful headdress instead of ashes,
the oil of gladness instead of mourning,
   the garment of praise instead of a faint spirit;
that they may be called oaks of righteousness,
   the planting of the LORD, that he may be glorified.[c]
⁴ They shall build up the ancient ruins;
   they shall raise up the former devastations;
they shall repair the ruined cities,
   the devastations of many generations.

____

____

____

____

____

LESSON 1: THE CONDITION OF THE WORLD & WHY WE ALL WILL EXPERIENCE DIFFICULTIES; AND WHAT THEN DOES GOD PROMISE TO OVERCOME THE WORLD?

The good news is that overcoming and deliverance happens now, regardless of what has happened in the past. It is for everyone—not just a few lucky ones. You have trouble and destructive patterns, and you need deliverance, but you have tried and tried, and it has never worked. Maybe you are older now and have really made a mess of things. Maybe you are in trouble with your marriage or in trouble with your finances or your business or with your kids. You doubt if this could ever be fully resolved so you might as well just live with it. This is the result of our sin nature. Jesus said, *The good news, the gospel, is that I can resolve it all.* How about now?

As we experience Him overcoming and delivering, we can tell others the good news that we now know is true. No matter how awful the situation, or how messy it might be, God can restore it. He's overcome this already, and He will restore to you the things that you've lost. This is the good news. Any issue you have—broken heartedness, sadness, mourning, loss, prison—He can restore it. Whether you are in prison because of your patterns, or things are ruined, or you have made ashes of stuff, rendering it worthless, He can restore it. If you have a lot of problems in your life, what does He say He will do? He will restore and overcome your circumstances. He will give you freedom and beauty. He will rebuild it. He will fulfill the promise He made.

What are the truths of what Christ has fulfilled for us? What is important to understand as to why He has the power to overcome? What is His purpose for overcoming? What does that mean to us personally?

Read Colossians 1:9–20:

9 And so, from the day we heard, we have not ceased to pray for you, asking that you may be filled with the knowledge of his will in all spiritual wisdom and understanding, 10 so as to walk in a manner worthy of the Lord, fully pleasing to him: bearing fruit in every good work and increasing in the knowledge of God; 11 being strengthened with all power, according to his glorious might, for all endurance and patience with joy; 12 giving thanks[a] to the Father, who has qualified you[b] to share in the inheritance of the saints in light. 13 He has delivered us from the domain of darkness and transferred us to the kingdom of his beloved Son, 14 in whom we have redemption, the forgiveness of sins. The Preeminence of Christ

> [15] He is the image of the invisible God, the firstborn of all creation. [16] For by[c] him all things were created, in heaven and on earth, visible and invisible, whether thrones or dominions or rulers or authorities—all things were created through him and for him. [17] And he is before all things, and in him all things hold together. [18] And he is the head of the body, the church. He is the beginning, the firstborn from the dead, that in everything he might be preeminent. [19] For in him all the fullness of God was pleased to dwell, [20] and through him to reconcile to himself all things, whether on earth or in heaven, making peace by the blood of his cross.

____

____

____

____

____

He says He has transferred you, moved you from the place of darkness (the world) into His what? Into the light, into His Kingdom. He brought you to the Kingdom.

Who created the Kingdom? Christ. With what did Christ create the Kingdom? His power, all things—both visible and invisible. It includes everything—even the heavenly host, including the demonic. It's all been created by Him—heaven and Earth. He spoke it by His work, His power, and it is why He is above all things.

If all things are subordinate to Him, which includes the trouble of your circumstances and the destructive patterns of your soul, what does it say about His ability to overcome it? It is complete and absolute—because He created it all. It's subordinated. The material things, as well as the things that are going on in the spirit world, are subordinated to His power. All the power is there in the Kingdom of God, which is why in verse 18, He says to let Him be preeminent. If we're going to be delivered, we have to learn to let Him be preeminent since He is the only one who can fulfill it. Could we do it on our own? No. How come? We don't have that power. Only He does. Only He is preeminent, and His purpose and heart for us is to reconcile all things, visible and invisible, back to Himself. This Greek word for reconcile means to restore to harmony all that was intended to be in the first place. He's implying that it's not going to be perfect like Adam and Eve, but He will give us the joy of the restored life. When? Now. Where? In this difficult place—even with our issues and troubled circumstances.

LESSON 1: THE CONDITION OF THE WORLD & WHY WE ALL WILL EXPERIENCE DIFFICULTIES; AND WHAT THEN DOES GOD PROMISE TO OVERCOME THE WORLD?

In order for us to overcome, what is necessary on our part? Why? What is the result if we fulfill our part?

> **Read Revelation 3:22:**
>
> [22] He who has an ear, let him hear what the Spirit says to the churches.'"

____

____

____

____

____

Overcoming. Who needs things to be overcome? All, but here it is speaking to believers. He says if He stands at the door knocks, what are you supposed to do? Open the door, let Him come in and then eat together, have dinner together, fellowship together. He's saying, _How about now? Are you going to let Me come in? Why are you out there in the world trying to do this yourself when I'm standing here ready to do it?_ He says if you do, you will become what? You will join Him in becoming an overcomer. That's what life is all about. Are you ever going to stop having trouble? No. Jesus said, _In the world, you're going to have trouble._ Why did Jesus say this? Because we live in an evil world. Are your patterns there? Yes, and they need to be delivered. They need to be transformed. He says, _If you allow Me, you'll actually join Me in the overcoming, and you will be then considered an overcomer—not by yourself._ He doesn't say good luck when you try to go off and overcome. He says to let Him do it, to join Him in being an overcomer, which is His desire for us to live the beautiful Covenant life—where He is going to bless us to make us a blessing. Let's look at the life of David to understand the depth of this.

In this history of Israel, what does Luke, the author of Acts, say about David? Why is that so important in our understanding of overcoming and deliverance? What does that mean to us personally?

Read Acts 13:13–20:

Paul and Barnabas at Antioch in Pisidia
[13] Now Paul and his companions set sail from Paphos and came to Perga in Pamphylia. And John left them and returned to Jerusalem, [14] but they went on from Perga and came to Antioch in Pisidia. And on the Sabbath day they went into the synagogue and sat down. [15] After the reading from the Law and the Prophets, the rulers of the synagogue sent a message to them, saying, "Brothers, if you have any word of encouragement for the people, say it." [16] So Paul stood up, and motioning with his hand said:

"Men of Israel and you who fear God, listen. [17] The God of this people Israel chose our fathers and made the people great during their stay in the land of Egypt, and with uplifted arm he led them out of it. [18] And for about forty years he put up with[a] them in the wilderness. [19] And after destroying seven nations in the land of Canaan, he gave them their land as an inheritance. [20] All this took about 450 years. And after that he gave them judges until Samuel the prophet.

____

____

____

____

____

Luke gives us a brief history of Israel, these grand epochs of Israel. In doing so, he mentions one person—David, a man after God's own heart, who was willing to do all His will. We will see that this is an important piece of overcoming. Do you have a heart to follow God's heart and do His will? That's what is spoken of David among all that broad history. It's remarkable, and we need to understand what that looks like so we can become an overcomer.

As Samuel was given the assignment of selecting God's new anointed king, what was important to God in this selection versus what Samuel thought? Why is this important as we walk with God to experience overcoming and deliverance?

Read 1 Samuel 16:6–7; 13:

6 When they came, he looked on Eliab and thought, "Surely the LORD'S anointed is before him." 7 But the Lord said to Samuel, "Do not look on his appearance or on the height of his stature, because I have rejected him. For the Lord sees not as man sees: man looks on the outward appearance, but the LORD looks on the heart."

13 Then Samuel took the horn of oil and anointed him in the midst of his brothers. And the Spirit of the LORD rushed upon David from that day forward. And Samuel rose up and went to Ramah.

Samuel reviewed all of Jesse's sons and even thought that some might be the one who God had wanted him to anoint. God said no to all of them and explained that Samuel was looking at the appearance while God looks at the heart.

Samuel asked Jesse if all of his sons were there. Jesse said there was one more, David, who was the youngest, but he was keeping the sheep. Samuel asked to have him come in. This is who God had selected. The Lord instructed Samuel to take the oil and anoint him—and the Spirit of the Lord came upon David. David was selected because Saul, who had been anointed as king, was doing his own thing, constantly working against the will of God. Saul did not have a heart to repent and let God guide him.

The message is very important for those of us who are in need of overcoming and deliverance. Are you trying to overcome on your own? Are you trying to resolve your issue? If yes, your ability to have things delivered or overcome are not possible, and you are working against God. Rather, do you have a desire to walk with God and let Him resolve this? Do you have a heart to follow God's heart and do all His will? This is critical as our beginning point toward overcoming and deliverance.

What did David say he wishes would be written in the book of life about him? Why is this significant for our relationship with God? What then is required of us?

Read Psalm 40:4–8:

4 Blessed is the man who makes
   the Lord his trust,
who does not turn to the proud,
   to those who go astray after a lie!
5 You have multiplied, O LORD my God,
   your wondrous deeds and your thoughts toward us;
   none can compare with you!
I will proclaim and tell of them,
   yet they are more than can be told.
6 In sacrifice and offering you have not delighted,
   but you have given me an open ear.[a]
Burnt offering and sin offering
   you have not required.
7 Then I said, "Behold, I have come;
   in the scroll of the book it is written of me:
8 I delight to do your will, O my God;
   your law is within my heart."

____

____

____

____

David says that He wanted to be honored and remembered in the Book of Life. His words were, *In all my life, I delighted to do the will of God.* He understood something significant. He knew that's where he could overcome, that's where he could be delivered. This leads to a question for all of us: Is that how you operate? May this be written of you—that you delighted to do God's will. This is your earmark for life.

Another indicator of the primary beginning point is that you have a heart to follow the will of God—to follow God and let Him be Your overcomer and deliverer. You can choose not to, which is what happened in Numbers 13 and 14 with the Israelites and Moses. Moses was sent to release the people, which happened through a miraculous crossing of the Red Sea. The waters parted, and they went through on dry ground—these miracles were for the benefit of two million people. Crossing the Red Sea took time, but what did God do during that time? He kept the army of the Egyptians stalled as they could not get past the column of fire He provided. The Egyptians were chasing them, but they couldn't go any farther because they couldn't get past the fire.

After the Israelites crossed, the water was released, and all the Egyptians died. All of Israel was saved, and it was a picture of salvation. You're saved and now free from the enemy camp. In this case, as soon as they were saved, God said He was giving them the Promised Land—a land of milk and honey, a land of houses, wells, produce, cattle, sheep—all of the things the Israelites needed were there. God said, *I'm going to deliver that to you, and nobody will be able to ever defeat you. Yes, there is an enemy already there in that same place, but I'll defeat the enemy.* He gave that promise. It was His will.

What were the reasons that the Israelites chose not to go to the Promise Land? What then was the impact of them experiencing overcoming and deliverance? Why? How does this relate to how we to address our difficult circumstances?

> **Read Numbers 13:25–14:4:**
>
> Report of the Spies
> [25] At the end of forty days they returned from spying out the land. [26] And they came to Moses and Aaron and to all the congregation of the people of Israel in the wilderness of Paran, at Kadesh. They brought back word to them and to all the congregation, and showed them the fruit of the land. [27] And they told him,

"We came to the land to which you sent us. It flows with milk and honey, and this is its fruit. [28] However, the people who dwell in the land are strong, and the cities are fortified and very large. And besides, we saw the descendants of Anak there. [29] The Amalekites dwell in the land of the Negeb. The Hittites, the Jebusites, and the Amorites dwell in the hill country. And the Canaanites dwell by the sea, and along the Jordan."

[30] But Caleb quieted the people before Moses and said, "Let us go up at once and occupy it, for we are well able to overcome it." [31] Then the men who had gone up with him said, "We are not able to go up against the people, for they are stronger than we are." [32] So they brought to the people of Israel a bad report of the land that they had spied out, saying, "The land, through which we have gone to spy it out, is a land that devours its inhabitants, and all the people that we saw in it are of great height. [33] And there we saw the Nephilim (the sons of Anak, who come from the Nephilim), and we seemed to ourselves like grasshoppers, and so we seemed to them."

The People Rebel

14 Then all the congregation raised a loud cry, and the people wept that night. [2] And all the people of Israel grumbled against Moses and Aaron. The whole congregation said to them, "Would that we had died in the land of Egypt! Or would that we had died in this wilderness! [3] Why is the Lord bringing us into this land, to fall by the sword? Our wives and our little ones will become a prey. Would it not be better for us to go back to Egypt?" [4] And they said to one another, "Let us choose a leader and go back to Egypt."

The spies who went out to review the conditions in the Promised Land reported that there was a powerful enemy there. The 10 spies said they were not able to fulfill God's will—meaning they were not able to overcome this. They believed they could not overcome this powerful enemy, and instead chose to grumble, complain, and say, in essence, that they were not going to go. They understood what God had said. They all understood God's will. But they still believed that they would not have the ability to overcome this obstacle. They then went through four common thoughts that people tend to think when faced with difficult circumstances:

1. If only. If only I would have made a different decision back then, I wouldn't be in this position now that I can't overcome. If only—and we even attribute that to other people—if only my parents hadn't treated me the way they treated me, I wouldn't have developed this pattern; if only my spouse were different; if only I had made better decisions, I would not be faced with this problem, and I would not be in this pickle—if only, if only, if only.

2. Why? Why has God brought us here? To kill us? In other words, you attribute your problem to whom? To God. This issue of my life, the circumstance of my life is real—how come He didn't make it or me different? How come I have an addiction? How come I have this problem with anger? He made me this way. Why did God make me this way? Why did God give me this issue in my life when He's supposed to be in control? Why is He making me suffer?

3. Wouldn't it be better if? This is where we try to control the situation. How about if I try to overcome this? Or, what if I just flee from the situation? Or maybe I'll just put up with it. What if I have a better plan, wouldn't it be better if I go my own way on this?

4. You do your own thing. You decide to act on the situation but then start moving on your own plan. You choose not to trust God's plan and go your own way.

This is referred to as a "bad report." This is contrary to what Joshua and Caleb did when they were faced with difficult circumstances.

LESSON 1: THE CONDITION OF THE WORLD & WHY WE ALL WILL EXPERIENCE DIFFICULTIES; AND WHAT THEN DOES GOD PROMISE TO OVERCOME THE WORLD?

In the next two sets of verses, please respond: What was different about Joshua and Caleb as they faced the same difficult circumstances as the Israelites? What difference did this make in their experiencing overcoming and deliverance? What role did faith play in this? What is the definition of faith? Why is this such an important element in us as we experience overcoming and deliverance?

Read Numbers 14:24:

24 But my servant Caleb, because he has a different spirit and has followed me fully, I will bring into the land into which he went, and his descendants shall possess it.

____

____

____

____

____

They had a different spirit. The difference in spirit is because they did what? They followed Him and believed that He would overcome. Caleb says, *Let's go. We can take it over.* The other people, those who did not trust in God's plan said, *Not only is it going to be bad, it's going to be awful.* They had opposite perspectives for the same circumstances in the same situation. Why? Let's go to Hebrews 11.

Read Hebrews 11:1–3:

By Faith

11 Now faith is the assurance of things hoped for, the conviction of things not seen. 2 For by it the people of old received their commendation. 3 By faith we understand that the universe was created by the word of God, so that what is seen was not made out of things that are visible.

____

____

____

____

____

As we previously read in Colossians—the world was created by Christ. How? He spoke it. That's why He can overcome—nothing is too difficult for Him because it's all subordinated to Him. He created it; He can change things in your life, and He can do a work in you to deliver you.

While the 10 spies had given a bad report, scripture says that the elders (referring to Joshua and Caleb) gave a good report. What's the difference between a good report and a bad report? How we respond to God and what He speaks. They all saw the same things, so they didn't deny the truth. They agreed that they had a big problem on their hands. Joshua and Caleb said, *Yes, but God said.* Since God said that's His will, Joshua and Caleb gave a good report because they believed what God said. *We're willing to go. Let's go. We don't know how. We don't know when. We don't know how this is all going to work. But God said, and we are willing to follow.* That is a good report. The bad report is, *We've got this awful thing. Yes, God said, but we're not going, we're not willing to go because we see the circumstance being too tough for us. It doesn't matter what God said. We don't care about His will. We've decided we are not following God or believing that this will be overcome.* We have a choice to make:

1. Are we willing to even hear God's will? Most people in the Christian world don't even think that's possible. *How can I know God's will when I can't hear what He has to speak? I guess I'll just do the best I can.* We must believe that He has a will, and He will speak that will to us in a way that we will hear it.

2. Do we have a heart to go—to follow His will? Why? Because He's preeminent. He's the one who can overcome. He's the one who can deliver. That is His heart for us.

In Isaiah 61, He says, *Every one of My children will receive and experience My offer to overcome and deliver. I can do it. It is what I've come to do. Are you going to follow Me or not?* What happened with the Israelites who chose not to follow Him, the ones who said they were not going and were not even willing to consider going? For 40 years, they wandered around, living a life of complete boredom and meaninglessness.

That's the essence of this issue—God will allow you to wander around and never experience His will—it is not automatic. The Israelites could not enter the Promised Land because they chose not to have a heart to follow, and they never experienced the overcoming. Think about the implication of that. The problems we need to overcome are going to get worse. We are never going to experience God's abundant life in a very difficult, troubled world if we accepted the bad report instead of believing and moving forward on the good report.

How did Saul and his fellow warriors respond to the overwhelmingly difficult circumstances? What was David's response? How then are we to address difficult circumstances in our lives? What can we then expect if we follow David's approach to overcoming and deliverance?

Read 1 Samuel 17:1–54:

David and Goliath

17 Now the Philistines gathered their armies for battle. And they were gathered at Socoh, which belongs to Judah, and encamped between Socoh and Azekah, in Ephes-dammim. [2] And Saul and the men of Israel were gathered, and encamped in the Valley of Elah, and drew up in line of battle against the Philistines. [3] And the Philistines stood on the mountain on the one side, and Israel stood on the mountain on the other side, with a valley between them. [4] And there came out from the camp of the Philistines a champion named Goliath of Gath, whose height was six[a] cubits[b] and a span. [5] He had a helmet of bronze on his head, and he was armed with a coat of mail, and the weight of the coat was five thousand shekels[c] of bronze. [6] And he had bronze armor on his legs, and a javelin of bronze slung between his shoulders. [7] The shaft of his spear was like a weaver's beam, and his spear's head weighed six hundred shekels of iron. And his shield-bearer went before him. [8] He stood and shouted to the ranks of Israel, "Why have you come out to draw up for battle? Am I not a Philistine, and are you not servants of Saul? Choose a man for yourselves, and let him come down to me. [9] If he is able to fight with me and kill me, then we will be your servants. But if I prevail against him and kill him, then you shall be our servants and serve us." 10 And the Philistine said, "I defy the ranks of Israel this day. Give me a man, that we may fight together." 11 When Saul and all Israel heard these words of the Philistine, they were dismayed and greatly afraid.

12 Now David was the son of an Ephrathite of Bethlehem in Judah, named Jesse, who had eight sons. In the days of Saul the man was already old and advanced in years.[d] 13 The three oldest sons of Jesse had followed Saul to the battle. And the names of his three sons who went to the battle were Eliab the firstborn, and next to him Abinadab, and the third Shammah. 14 David was the youngest. The three eldest followed Saul, 15 but David went back and forth from Saul to feed his father's sheep at Bethlehem. 16 For forty days the Philistine came forward and took his stand, morning and evening.

17 And Jesse said to David his son, "Take for your brothers an ephah[e] of this parched grain, and these ten loaves, and carry them quickly to the camp to your brothers. 18 Also take these ten cheeses to the commander of their thousand. See if your brothers are well, and bring some token from them." 19 Now Saul and they and all the men of Israel were in the Valley of Elah, fighting with the Philistines. 20 And David rose early in the morning and left the sheep with a keeper and took the provisions and went, as Jesse had commanded him. And he came to the encampment as the host was going out to the battle line, shouting the war cry. 21 And Israel and the Philistines drew up for battle, army against army. 22 And David left the things in charge of the keeper of the baggage and ran to the ranks and went and greeted his brothers. 23 As he talked with them, behold, the champion, the Philistine of Gath, Goliath by name, came up out of the ranks of the Philistines and spoke the same words as before. And David heard him.

24 All the men of Israel, when they saw the man, fled from him and were much afraid. 25 And the men of Israel said, "Have you seen this man who has come up? Surely he has come up to defy Israel. And the king will enrich the man who kills him with great riches and will give him his daughter and make his father's house free in Israel." 26 And David said to the men who stood by him, "What shall be done for the man who kills this Philistine and takes away the reproach from Israel? For who is this uncircumcised Philistine, that he should defy the armies of the living God?" 27 And the people answered him in the same way, "So shall it be done to the man who kills him."

28 Now Eliab his eldest brother heard when he spoke to the men. And Eliab's anger was kindled against David, and he said, "Why have you come down? And with whom have you left those few sheep in the wilderness? I know your presumption and the evil of your heart, for you have come down to see the battle." 29 And David said, "What have I done now? Was it not but a word?" 30 And he turned away from him toward another, and spoke in the same way, and the people answered him again as before.

31 When the words that David spoke were heard, they repeated them before Saul, and he sent for him. 32 And David said to Saul, "Let no man's heart fail because of him. Your servant will go and fight with this Philistine." 33 And Saul said to David, "You are not able to go against this Philistine to fight with him, for you are but a youth, and he has been a man of war from his youth." 34 But David said to Saul, "Your servant used to keep sheep for his father. And when there came a lion, or a bear, and took a lamb from the flock, 35 I went after him and struck him and delivered it out of his mouth. And if he arose against me, I caught him by his beard and struck him and killed him. 36 Your servant has struck down both lions and bears, and this uncircumcised Philistine shall be like one of them, for he has defied the armies of the living God." 37 And David said, "The Lord who delivered me from the paw of the lion and from the paw of the bear will deliver me from the hand of this Philistine." And Saul said to David, "Go, and the Lord be with you!"

38 Then Saul clothed David with his armor. He put a helmet of bronze on his head and clothed him with a coat of mail, 39 and David strapped his sword over his armor. And he tried in vain to go, for he had not tested them. Then David said to Saul, "I cannot go with these, for I have not tested them." So David put them off. 40 Then he took his staff in his hand and chose five smooth stones from the brook and put them in his shepherd's pouch. His sling was in his hand, and he approached the Philistine.

41 And the Philistine moved forward and came near to David, with his shield-bearer in front of him. 42 And when the Philistine looked and saw David, he disdained him, for he was but a youth, ruddy and handsome in appearance. 43 And the Philistine said to David, "Am I a dog, that you come to me with sticks?" And the Philistine cursed David by his gods. 44 The Philistine said to David, "Come to me, and I will give your flesh to the birds of the air and to the beasts of the field." 45 Then David said to the Philistine, "You come to me with a sword and with a spear and with a javelin, but I come to you in the name of the Lord of hosts, the God of the armies of Israel, whom you have

defied. [46] This day the Lord will deliver you into my hand, and I will strike you down and cut off your head. And I will give the dead bodies of the host of the Philistines this day to the birds of the air and to the wild beasts of the earth, that all the earth may know that there is a God in Israel, [47] and that all this assembly may know that the Lord saves not with sword and spear. For the battle is the Lord's, and he will give you into our hand."

[48] When the Philistine arose and came and drew near to meet David, David ran quickly toward the battle line to meet the Philistine. [49] And David put his hand in his bag and took out a stone and slung it and struck the Philistine on his forehead. The stone sank into his forehead, and he fell on his face to the ground.

[50] So David prevailed over the Philistine with a sling and with a stone, and struck the Philistine and killed him. There was no sword in the hand of David. [51] Then David ran and stood over the Philistine and took his sword and drew it out of its sheath and killed him and cut off his head with it. When the Philistines saw that their champion was dead, they fled. [52] And the men of Israel and Judah rose with a shout and pursued the Philistines as far as Gath[f] and the gates of Ekron, so that the wounded Philistines fell on the way from Shaaraim as far as Gath and Ekron. [53] And the people of Israel came back from chasing the Philistines, and they plundered their camp. [54] And David took the head of the Philistine and brought it to Jerusalem, but he put his armor in his tent.

____

____

____

____

____

During this time, battles were fought by armies facing off on opposite ends of a designated location. Each side brought their warriors to engage in battle, and whoever lost had to surrender to the winner, or the winner would just take them over. It was hand-to-hand combat, and the army with the most people usually won. Women and children would not participate in the battles, and if one side didn't show up to fight, the other would come and kill everybody.

For this particular battle, Saul and his army go to En-Gedi, south of Jerusalem, where they encounter Goliath. He comes out says, *Why don't we just skip all this killing stuff? You pick somebody to come against me* (he's eight or nine feet tall and probably weighs three or four hundred pounds), *and whoever wins between us will then have the other army surrender to the winner, and it will avoid all this killing.* The Philistine continued, *I defy the Army of Israel this day. Give me a man that we may fight together.* He lays out the deal. What was the response of Saul and his men? They were dismayed and greatly afraid. Why? They believed that nobody could defeat Goliath. This is it. This problem is too big.

We often get into this same mode—We have a problem. We look at the problem. We can't see a way to get through it. It is going to be too much. Your imagination goes to the worst-case scenario of this issue, and you project that's what is going to happen to you. Saul and his army were greatly afraid and dismayed. *Dismay* means there is no way out of this. Why Saul was dismayed was because He had no solution in his own mind for this situation; and during this time of fear and dismay, he failed to do the one thing that could bring resolution. He didn't go to God. He had already concluded that this problem was too big and that he would have to overcome it on his own, which he couldn't.

When Jesse sends David to the battle to find out how his brothers were doing, he questions what was going on there. At that time, Goliath came out and repeated the challenge, which David heard. He inquired as to what would be done for the one who took care of this problem and was told that the king will give him great riches, will give him his daughter, and will give his father's house exemption from all taxes. He kept trying to sweeten the pot. Saul had been asking if anybody wanted to go, but the only response he received was no.

David then says, *Who is this uncircumcised Philistine that he should defy the army of the living God?* He didn't see a giant. He just saw a guy who was defying God. He saw a guy who thought he could defy the army of the living God. There's the key the statement. As you're coming up against adversity, things to be overcome, the issues of your heart, you are to approach this with a heart that knows that God will overcome. How dare this come against you and defy you, who is part of the army of the living God? How dare this? Why could David make that statement?

1. He had a heart to follow God in the very beginning.

2. David had situations earlier in life where he personally had experienced God delivering and overcoming—the lion and the bear—what God had promised.

3. He was a student of the scriptures. He knew that God had promised the Covenant—He has protected and delivered the land and peoples of Israel because of His Covenant promise. Remember Joshua and Caleb? What did He say? I'm giving you this land, and no one will be able to defeat you. That was the promise. David understood that. He said, *We're living in the Covenant, so how dare he defy the army of the living God.* Why? Because we're living in the Covenant, and God has promised this to us. It still applies. David, having the heart to follow God, went to belief and trust in the character and Word of God. He was a man after God's own heart.

We need to understand that the Covenant still exists today. He is going to bless us to make us a blessing. These are things that are absolute. They're promises that are given to us. When we walk into a situation, the first thing that God wants us to say is, *How dare this come against me?* We might not know the solution yet, but this is where we start. The difference between David and Saul is faith versus fear—going to God or trying to figure this out ourselves or going to resignation? Following God's promises or not?

David was asked to try on Saul's armor, which he did, but it didn't fit. Why? It's not the way God was asking David to join him in His work. It's not you putting on somebody else's system. It is simply following what God has taught you and now speaks to you. David goes out with his rocks and his sling, and the Philistine said to him, *Am I a dog that you come at me with sticks?* The Philistine cursed David by his gods and then said to him, *Come to me, and I will give your flesh to the birds in the air and the beasts of the field.* Then David said, *You come to me with a sword, a spear, and a javelin. Yes, I know you have these armaments that are way bigger than mine. But this day I come to you in the name of the Lord of Hosts, the God of the armies of Israel, whom you have defied this day. The Lord will deliver you into my hand, and I will strike you and take your head from you. This day, I will give the carcasses of the camp of the Philistines to the birds of the air and the wild beasts of the Earth. And all the Earth may know that there is a God in Israel. They shall know that the Lord does not save with sword and spear—for the battle is the Lord's, and He will give you into our hands.*

So, there it is. When you have a problem there are three basic steps:

1. How dare this come against me? I don't need to put up with this. God's going to overcome it. Why? Because He promises that.

2. Seek the Father: How would You have me go? In the way that You have fit and ordained for me to join You in your work. I understand that I am not just to ask You to take care of it in the way that I think, but that Your way is going to involve me personally. You're the one who will be called to exercise authority, belief, and faith—and to receive wisdom about what is going on that is important for my understanding of Your promise, Your purpose and what is important for this to be resolved; I'm willing to go into the battle.

3. When I come to battle, I'm coming at it in the name of the Lord, who will deliver this thing into my hand. I'm going to follow Him, and He's going to do the work. His Covenant stands, and I can rely on this and move forward with confidence and see the mighty work of God that overcomes and delivers.

As we complete this first lesson, we understand something about the world. Jesus said, *I've overcome it. I've come to restore you.* I'm preeminent. We have the opportunity to follow Him. Do you have a heart to follow Him? Like David? Like Joshua and Caleb? Yes, you are going to have problems, *but let God handle them.* Let Him be preeminent and overcome your problems.

As we continue with Lesson 2 in *Overcoming and Deliverance: A Study of the Life of David*, we've learned that Christ said that in the world we are going to have problems to overcome. We are going to have patterns in our life that are soul issues—what we call soul wounds. But He says, *I can overcome it and deliver you because I'm preeminent. I've overcome the world. My heart is to restore things—your issues and soul wounds—back to the abundant life. I promise you that I will overcome them, and I will deliver you from these wounds.*

As we also learned, the question to each of us is: Do you have a heart to follow? You have a choice to make. Do you want to follow God's plan and experience what He has in store for you, or have you decided that the circumstances are too tough and you either have to try to fix them on your own or just give up on them entirely? He says, *Come with Me, and we can experience the overcoming and the deliverance together.*

We learned from David, who was a man after God's own heart, that when Goliath was coming against the nation and against him—he stood against Goliath in the name of God and proclaimed, *How dare he defy God!* He then went into battle and experienced the overcoming.

After the victory with Goliath, David joined Saul in his court as a leader of battle. He began developing his leadership skills, and people started to notice. They started saying that David leads and wins over ten thousand, but Saul, not as many. Upon hearing this, Saul became jealous and then fearful that David was going to replace him as king—especially since Samuel had already informed Saul that God was going to replace him. Saul decided that he was not going to let that happen and set out to kill David—and so David fled. David is on the run, and it's personal. He is all by himself when he winds up in a cave.

David is feeling greatly discouraged and basically says to God in Psalm 142, *I thought You said that I was supposed to be king—not only am I not king, but I'm also not even living at home, I'm not enjoying life, I'm alone. All of this awful stuff happening*

> "As we also learned, the question to each of us is: Do you have a heart to follow?"

to me, and I hate being in the caves by myself. Woe is me. All of this is happening to him, and he gets discouraged. Many believers can relate to feeling this way, like you've tried and tried to resolve your issues but you cannot. You thought God was in control, but if He's in control, wouldn't your life be good? Or at least shouldn't it be better than this? But instead, your problems just keep compounding on themselves, and you get discouraged. David was discouraged, but the story does not end there. There is good news ahead.

What happened that led to David being alone, living in caves? How did David feel being alone in the caves? What did God do then to bring hope and encouragement back to David? Why is this such an important part of overcoming and deliverance?

Read Psalm 142:

You Are My Refuge
A Maskil[a] of David, when he was in the cave. A Prayer.
142 With my voice I cry out to the LORD;
    with my voice I plead for mercy to the LORD.
² I pour out my complaint before him;
    I tell my trouble before him.
³ When my spirit faints within me,
    you know my way!
In the path where I walk
    they have hidden a trap for me.
⁴ Look to the right and see:
    there is none who takes notice of me;
no refuge remains to me;
    no one cares for my soul.
⁵ I cry to you, O LORD;
    I say, "You are my refuge,
    my portion in the land of the living."
⁶ Attend to my cry,
    for I am brought very low!
Deliver me from my persecutors,
    for they are too strong for me!

LESSON 2:
WHAT ARE THE DIFFERENT ELEMENTS OF GOD PROVIDING OVERCOMING AND DELIVERANCE?

> [7] Bring me out of prison,
>   that I may give thanks to your name!
> The righteous will surround me,
>   for you will deal bountifully with me.

Read 1 Samuel 22:1–5:

David at the Cave of Adullam

22 David departed from there and escaped to the cave of Adullam. And when his brothers and all his father's house heard it, they went down there to him. [2] And everyone who was in distress, and everyone who was in debt, and everyone who was bitter in soul,[a] gathered to him. And he became commander over them. And there were with him about four hundred men.

[3] And David went from there to Mizpeh of Moab. And he said to the king of Moab, "Please let my father and my mother stay[b] with you, till I know what God will do for me." [4] And he left them with the king of Moab, and they stayed with him all the time that David was in the stronghold. [5] Then the prophet Gad said to David, "Do not remain in the stronghold; depart, and go into the land of Judah." So David departed and went into the forest of Hereth.

____

____

____

____

David is very discouraged, complaining, and wondering how this had all happened. *How is this supposed to be my life? Why?* In the middle of this discouragement, what does God do? He sends his family to go find him. They did not have a way to simply go to where he was. They did not know his exact location and had to go from cave to cave to cave until God led them to the right one. When they showed up, what did that do for David? Just seeing them gave him encouragement. He was no longer alone. They were there for him, just as God was there for him, and just as God is here for us today. God is here, bringing the body together to walk with you through your adversity—which is the purpose of the body of Christ. David now had fellowship, encouragement, and a renewed sense of hope that God was leading him.

As you consider having fellowship with other spiritual believers—your spouse, friend(s), inner circle, small group—how can you seek together God's will? Why does God assure us that we can always hear, receive, and understand His will? Why is this so important in overcoming and deliverance?

Read Ephesians 4:1–6; 11–16:

Unity in the Body of Christ
4 I therefore, a prisoner for the Lord, urge you to walk in a manner worthy of the calling to which you have been called, ² with all humility and gentleness, with patience, bearing with one another in love, ³ eager to maintain the unity of the Spirit in the bond of peace. ⁴ There is one body and one Spirit—just as you were called to the one hope that belongs to your call— ⁵ one Lord, one faith, one baptism, 6 one God and Father of all, who is over all and through all and in all.

We are to make every effort, which in the Greek says, work really, really, really, really hard to get to the unity of the faith. Your unity is with whom? The Spirit. The family that God brought to David lifted him out of his discouragement. We are not to get discouraged and go off trying to figure things out on your own, but rather work with your spouse, work with your family, work with your inner circle or small group to stay together. Make every effort to go to the unity of the Spirit together to discover and then follow God's will. We all are to speak the truth and not be afraid to say when we are discouraged or have an issue or question or a problem that we need help with. Then, in fellowship, go seek the Father together. What does He have to say about this? We already know about God's Covenant. God will restore this. God will overcome this. We don't need to live with that anymore. We don't know the answer, but we can stand together until we get to the answer.

The simple act of standing next to somebody, coming alongside them, and saying, *Let's go get God's answer because we know He'll deliver it,* is enough to pull someone out of the hopelessness that they might be feeling. Our role is to speak the truth. Here's what God's saying, and here are the things that He has absolutely promised. God promised the Covenant, where He will bless you to make you a blessing. Jesus said, *In the world, you're going to have trouble, but don't fret, I've overcome the world, and I'm going to restore you.* Do not stay in discouragement or resignation, complaining. Instead, go talk with God and receive what He has to say as He promises resolution.

We stand together and build each other up to get to the unity of the faith. We are not called to just let people live in discouragement and fear. If you are going to help people live without discouragement and fear, what's important for you? It is important that you are not living that way. Does that mean you won't have trouble? No, but you know what to do with it. You'll gain confidence even when you might get a little bit discouraged. You will know that you need your spouse or a friend, or your small group to come alongside you. You'll stay there together strengthening and building up each other.

As David is gaining hope and confidence because of his family joining him, other people discover where he is, and they come and join him, too. Who else shows up? Others who are discouraged—in debt with no ability to pay, uneducated—the down-and-outers. Four hundred of them showed up.

Why did God send these people? God told David that if he was going to be king, it starts with these guys. *This is your army.* We can just imagine what David thought. *They don't know anything at all—especially about going to battle and going to war—they all are in trouble, and they're all sad, discouraged. What the heck are you sending me these guys for?* God said that David would see what He was about ready to do. Are you going to be faithful? Just like the Parable of the Talents in Matthew 25, are you going to be faithful in small things? If so, He'll give you greater things.

In other words, God says, *David, your path to being king starts here. You be faithful to these guys. I've given them to you.* He receives that message, and his family reinforced it. David went from being alone to having his family join him to now having these 400 men to train. Together, all of them leave the caves and go to Mizpah of Moab, which is pleasant—living back in a city with normal life. David goes to the king and asks if it is OK if he and his family stay there. He wants to stay there until God tells him what to do, and he needs his family to confirm God's will. So he asks the king if they can stay with him until he knows God's will. The king agrees to let him stay, and David and his family, together, went to the Father and sought His will.

The prophet comes to David and says, *Don't stay here, you've got to go—now.* David then received what He sought together with his family—God's will. Does he know all of God's will? No, just the next step. That's it. He learned that he couldn't stay there. Even though it was pleasant and he likely wanted to stay there, he had to go back to the caves. His family helped him confirm that, and he let them go. He knew God's will and had a whole new group of 400 around him who would go with him and help confirm God's will.

Think about what happened to David. He was alone, discouraged, and really upset. God brought his family to him. In doing so, God gave David the encouragement that he needed. *Do you have a heart to seek My will? They'll confirm it. I'm showing you My will—and I know for the moment it makes no sense to you, but I'm showing you My will through confirmation as you together go to the unity of the Spirit. Even though you would rather step into your call to be king, I am asking you to be faithful to those whom I'm sending you. Train them—stay in Mizpah with your family and them until you receive My will for your next step. What's the next step?* David had to leave the comfort of the city and return to the caves.

What is David understanding, what is he receiving from God? He is receiving and understanding the fact that the story isn't over. He is still going to be king, but it's just going to take a few steps to get there. This is step one—let's go. David went from discouragement to what? Being filled with hope and excitement. He understood.

As you read through this story of David at Keilah, what did you notice about how David sought and received God's will? What did David do when his men disagreed with what he believed was God's will? Why is this so important in working together with our inner circle? David could have assumed that certain things were expected when he learned that Saul was coming after him in Keilah, but instead, how did he approach the situation? Why is this so important in following God into His steps of overcoming and deliverance?

Read 1 Samuel 23:1–13:

David Saves the City of Keilah

23 Now they told David, "Behold, the Philistines are fighting against Keilah and are robbing the threshing floors." [2] Therefore David inquired of the LORD, "Shall I go and attack these Philistines?" And the LORD said to David, "Go and attack the Philistines and save Keilah." [3] But David's men said to him, "Behold, we are afraid here in Judah; how much more then if we go to Keilah against the armies of the Philistines?" [4] Then David inquired of the LORD again. And the LORD answered him, "Arise, go down to Keilah, for I will give the Philistines into your hand." [5] And David and his men went to Keilah and fought with the Philistines and brought away their livestock and struck them with a great blow.

So David saved the inhabitants of Keilah.

[6] When Abiathar the son of Ahimelech had fled to David to Keilah, he had come down with an ephod in his hand. [7] Now it was told Saul that David had come to Keilah. And Saul said, "God has given him into my hand, for he has shut himself in by entering a town that has gates and bars." [8] And Saul summoned all the people to war, to go down to Keilah, to besiege David and his men. [9] David knew that Saul was plotting harm against him. And he said to Abiathar the priest, "Bring the ephod here." [10] Then David said, "O LORD, the God of Israel, your servant has surely heard that Saul seeks to come to Keilah, to destroy the city on my account. [11] Will the men of Keilah surrender me into his hand? Will Saul come down, as your servant has heard? O LORD, the God of Israel, please tell your servant." And the Lord said, "He will come down." [12] Then David said, "Will the men of Keilah surrender me and my men into the hand of Saul?" And the LORD said, "They will surrender you." [13] Then David and his men, who were about six hundred, arose and departed from Keilah, and they went wherever they could go. When Saul was told that David had escaped from Keilah, he gave up the expedition.

David and his men are back in the caves hiding. David is training them when they find out that a nearby city, Keilah in Israel, is being attacked by the Philistines who are trying to overrun that town. David knows that the city under attack is not too far from where they are. He goes to God and asks what he should do. *Are You asking me to go and assist them? Is this our first opportunity to exercise our training for war?* God said, *Yes, go.* So, David says to his men, *We're going to Keilah to defeat the Philistines.*

David's men respond saying, *There's no way we're doing that. That doesn't make any sense at all.* They had two reasons they gave David:

1. They argued that the Philistines were way stronger than they were. They believed they were nothing, and there was no way they could successfully accomplish this task.

2. If they did go to Keilah, Saul would find out and would go there and kill them. Saul had been after them the whole time—so it didn't make any sense to expose themselves there. They simply did not want to go.

This is likely a normal situation for us. As you're seeking God's will and you're attempting to confirm that with your spouse, with your friends, with your small group, the first reaction can be what? Opposition. It doesn't make sense to them. They do not agree or support going that route. What then did David do when his men, his inner circle, said they didn't agree and that it didn't make sense to them? David said, let's go back to God together.

Now we know something. Does God mind confirming what He has already said? No. And He'll show that to the other party, which is what we read in Ephesians—He will get you to unity of the Spirit to confirm His will, 100 percent of the time, all the time. If you have a heart to go and receive, He will confirm it one way or the other—this included David. Maybe he didn't hear Him correctly? What could David have said to his men?

1. This is what God told me, so we're doing it. There would not be confirmation, and his men would go under duress, with no enthusiasm.

2. Yes, I could see that we're going there to get killed. I agree this is not a good idea, and it doesn't make any sense. Since it doesn't make any sense, let's not go.

Rather, David said, *Let's go to God together, even though you disagree with me, let's all hear what He has to say.* David knows that God will confirm it one way or the other, and they will come to unity.

When your spouse disagrees with you or when your friends disagree or your small group disagrees, do you let them dictate how you move forward and or do you move forward anyways? What should you do? Go to God. If you are in disagreement, you don't yet know God's will. It's OK that we disagree, but we need to keep pursuing it. The Holy Spirit lives in each of us, and He will help us get to unity. He's promises to get us to the answer, but there is a requirement. Both of us have to have a heart after God's own heart to seek His will. Do you have that? We will together receive it.

David and his men go to God together asking if He wants them to go to Keilah. God says, Yes. I'm telling you—yes. He also shares that He will deliver them. You go to Keilah, and I'll deliver you. David and his men hear it, acknowledge it, and understand it. We got it. Let's go. We all heard it. Let's go now. Unity gives you the confidence that God's going to do this. We can go safely and know victory is being given to us by God.

David and his army go to Keilah, defeat the Philistines, and save the town. David and his men take up residence in Keilah and are enjoying all the perks of living in the city instead of in the caves. They have beds, food, games, fun, fellowship, baths, and are enjoying life. They're saying, This is good. But, then Saul finds out that they're in this town. Since Keilah was surrounded by a small mountain, the only way in and out was through one gate, so Saul is certain he will find David. He knows he is there and believes that he can't escape.

By this time, David has 600 men, but Saul has thousands. Saul believes he's got him because there's no way they can win or defeat his army—he has too many numbers in place that David cannot escape. Saul even says that God has given David into his hand—which he attributes to God. He isn't going to God, but he is attributing things to God, which happens a lot for believers. God is doing this, God is doing that, God said this, God said that, but they never actually heard it. They just assume it or want it and attribute it to that.

Saul is coming, but through the role of the Holy Spirit, David was given a heads-up. *Something's about to happen here. David, I know you're enjoying this city, but there is something about to happen that you need to be aware of—there is a potential adversity.*

Given that David defeated Goliath and that God brought him to Keilah where he and his army defeated the Philistines, what could he have assumed? That God could do it again. He knew that God brought them there and they wanted to stay there. From that, he assumed that God's will was for them to stay there. This is what happens in our decision making. Because of the circumstances, we assume the next thing is the one that makes sense to us and is attractive to us—*We'll take it from here because it makes sense.*

Rather, what did David do? He checked in. *Father, here we are. I have two questions. Is Saul really coming?* If the answer was *no*, that would be the end of the discussion. He would not listen to or believe the intelligence that he was getting. But when he asked God if Saul was really coming, He said, *Yes, he's coming.*

Since David had just saved the men of Keilah, he assumed that they were going to help him defeat Saul. But instead of moving forward with that assumption, he asked God if they were going to hand him over to Saul to save themselves. God said, *Yes, they are. You have to leave.* Even though they liked living there, God told him to leave and go back to the cave. Was that preferable to David? No, but that was the instruction he was given. *If you don't leave, you are going to be defeated. I'm telling you, My will in this case isn't for you to stand and fight. If you stay, you're going to be defeated. My will is for you to exit.* And they do.

Did David ever get handed over by the men of Keilah? No, David left, so this situation never occurred at all. But this begs the question: How did God know since it never happened? Because He knows the outcome for whatever choices we make. He knows everything. He fully knows the potential of what's going to happen if you choose this path or that path. It would be similar to our understanding today of virtual reality. It doesn't really happen, but here's what would happen if it played out. God knows the consequence if David rejected His will and decided to stay there. He let David know the consequence so there were no questions about whether or not he should leave. David had to leave. The situation never happened, but he got his instruction from God, who did see it. How fantastic it is that every decision you have, God says, *I know the outcome, and my path is better.* When decisions or choices don't make sense, go together and ask what God has to say about it. He will reveal it to you in a way that you will understand. When will God respond to you? All the time. God's will is very specific and very intentional—personal to each situation.

Because it is specific to each of us individually, at any point in our life, we could be going down the path that God has confirmed when He turns us around and has us head in a different direction. He might have us do something completely opposite. In your mind, it doesn't make sense, and you question why He would have you go down that path as opposed to going down this new path in the first place. There are two reasons that God gives:

1. Timing. This new path wasn't ready. He needed you to pursue something different in order to prepare the path for you. He needed you to delay. He purposely put you down this path for a reason.

2. He is teaching you things. There are things you needed to learn that were important for you to understand before He led you onto the right path.

David had a heart to follow God, and he was continuously asking God what his next step should be. *What should I do now? Now what?*

As we seek God's will to walk onto His path of overcoming and deliverance, what are we needing to seek? What does this mean practically? Why is this so important to following God?

Read John 3:16–21:

For God So Loved the World

[16] "For God so loved the world,[a] that he gave his only Son, that whoever believes in him should not perish but have eternal life. [17] For God did not send his Son into the world to condemn the world, but in order that the world might be saved through him. [18] Whoever believes in him is not condemned, but whoever does not believe is condemned already, because he has not believed in the name of the only Son of God. [19] And this is the judgment: the light has come into the world, and people loved the darkness rather than the light because their works were evil. [20] For everyone who does wicked things hates the light and does not come to the light, lest his works should be exposed. [21] But whoever does what is true comes to the light, so that it may be clearly seen that his works have been carried out in God."

____

____

____

____

____

Christ says, *If you're going to follow Me, come to the light.* The truth. Like David, we should always be asking God what is next, what the truth is, how we come to the light. He said, *If you don't come to the light, you are in darkness. It's not a neutral thing. If you don't come and pursue My truth, you are in darkness.* If David had assumed certain things and had never come to the light, he then would have been in darkness—and would have remained in darkness, hampered by not knowing or receiving God's will—which in the situation with Keilah saved his life.

As we go into this next story, we will learn how to overcome and process through those who are opposing you and are unfairly harming you—coming against you. This is a common scheme of the enemy as we seek to overcome trouble—which is oftentimes caused by people close to us. The trouble could be caused by fellow Christians, who are doing things that just are not right—who are opposing us. It could be caused by family members, your small group, others at church, employees, and bosses. There's lots of potential for the many people around us to oppose us because they are self-centered—which is the norm of the world. But our position, interest, and desire are not to be in agreement or surrendered to them—which can cause great conflict and potential for hurt.

Describe the process of how David handled conflict and Saul coming after him, especially since he could have taken things into his own hands by serving justice himself. What did God teach him, and why was this so important to learn as we experience conflict all the time?

Read 1 Samuel 24:1–22:

David Spares Saul's Life

24 [a] When Saul returned from following the Philistines, he was told, "Behold, David is in the wilderness of Engedi." [2] Then Saul took three thousand chosen men out of all Israel and went to seek David and his men in front of the Wildgoats' Rocks. [3] And he came to the sheepfolds by the way, where there was a cave, and Saul went in to relieve himself.[b] Now David and his men were sitting in the innermost parts of the cave. [4] And the men of David said to him, "Here is the day of which the LORD said to you, 'Behold, I will give your enemy into your hand, and you shall do to him as it shall seem good to you.'" Then David arose and stealthily cut off a corner of Saul's robe. [5] And afterward David's heart struck him, because he had cut off a corner of Saul's robe. [6] He said to his men, "The LORD forbid that I should do this thing to my lord, the Lord's anointed, to put out my hand against him, seeing he is the Lord's anointed." [7] So David persuaded his men with these words and did not permit them to attack Saul. And Saul rose up and left the cave and went on his way.

[8] Afterward David also arose and went out of the cave, and called after Saul, "My lord the king!" And when Saul looked behind him, David bowed with his face to the earth and paid homage. [9] And David said to Saul, "Why do you listen to the words of men who say, 'Behold, David seeks your harm'? [10] Behold, this day your eyes have seen how the LORD gave you today into my hand in the cave. And some told me to kill you, but I spared you.[c] I said, 'I will not put

out my hand against my lord, for he is the Lord's anointed.' [11] See, my father, see the corner of your robe in my hand. For by the fact that I cut off the corner of your robe and did not kill you, you may know and see that there is no wrong or treason in my hands. I have not sinned against you, though you hunt my life to take it. [12] May the LORD judge between me and you, may the LORD avenge me against you, but my hand shall not be against you. [13] As the proverb of the ancients says, 'Out of the wicked comes wickedness.' But my hand shall not be against you. [14] After whom has the king of Israel come out? After whom do you pursue? After a dead dog! After a flea! [15] May the LORD therefore be judge and give sentence between me and you, and see to it and plead my cause and deliver me from your hand."

[16] As soon as David had finished speaking these words to Saul, Saul said, "Is this your voice, my son David?" And Saul lifted up his voice and wept. [17] He said to David, "You are more righteous than I, for you have repaid me good, whereas I have repaid you evil. [18] And you have declared this day how you have dealt well with me, in that you did not kill me when the Lord put me into your hands. [19] For if a man finds his enemy, will he let him go away safe? So may the Lord reward you with good for what you have done to me this day. [20] And now, behold, I know that you shall surely be king, and that the kingdom of Israel shall be established in your hand. [21] Swear to me therefore by the Lord that you will not cut off my offspring after me, and that you will not destroy my name out of my father's house." [22] And David swore this to Saul. Then Saul went home, but David and his men went up to the stronghold.

____
____
____
____
____

One of the many beautiful things about the Bible is that it shows things as they are and does not sanitize the truth. David saw Saul go into the cave to do what? Relieve himself. Saul goes in to relieve himself, and David and his men see this because they are hiding there in the cave. It was a large cave, and Saul didn't know they were there. David's men thought this must be the opportunity that God gave

David to kill Saul. It was the opportunity for him to execute justice—to kill him easily and solve all of their problems. David agrees, but as he is about to take the matter into his own hands, what happens to him? The Holy Spirit says, *I know what you're about to do, but I am not giving you permission*. This is called checking of the Spirit. What seemed like a good idea turned to a lack of peace and a troubling—it is God saying, *No, what you are planning is not of Me*.

David, instead, cuts off a corner of Saul's robe. He's right next to him and cuts the corner of his robe—which Saul likely took off. He then goes back to his men and explains that he couldn't follow through—even though he knows that they all think it is a good idea. He couldn't follow through because the Holy Spirit has checked him and said, *No, this is not His will*.

David then goes into a conversation with God and asks Him a simple question: Why not? God says, *Because this isn't yours to do. This is Mine to do. I'll establish justice. Vengeance is Mine, not yours. Even though you had this opportunity right before you, do not take it into your own hands*. The Spirit had checked David, and David listened to what He had to say and understood.

David then goes out to Saul and says, I could have killed you. You see that I have a corner of the robe that I cut off with a knife—which I easily could have used on you. I didn't because God said to let Him judge between you and me. And we'll just see what happens. My heart isn't to avenge anything of you, so I'm not coming after you at all. I'm trying to resolve this. Would you have a heart to do that with me at the moment?

After hearing this, Saul said, Thank you for not killing me. When you do become king—which is interesting that he acknowledged this—don't let my family, my lineage get destroyed. David agrees, and they part ways.

Following this exchange, Saul changed his mind and decided to attempt to kill David anyway. He kept going after him, constantly trying to kill him. The hurt never stopped, nor did the opposition. It looked like they were reconciled, but they really weren't. David could have asked God why this was happening. He could have complained about how they were not reconciled as Saul was still trying to harm him. He thought God told him to not worry because vengeance is His. Why was he still being pursued by Saul?

As you process through this next set of two verses, identify the important truths of what God speaks about how to respond when people continually oppose and hurt you. How are we to live these out in our practical lives? What is the result for us if we do?

Read Romans 12:9–21:

Marks of the True Christian

⁹ Let love be genuine. Abhor what is evil; hold fast to what is good. 10 Love one another with brotherly affection. Outdo one another in showing honor. ¹¹ Do not be slothful in zeal, be fervent in spirit,[a] serve the Lord. ¹² Rejoice in hope, be patient in tribulation, be constant in prayer. ¹³ Contribute to the needs of the saints and seek to show hospitality.

¹⁴ Bless those who persecute you; bless and do not curse them. ¹⁵ Rejoice with those who rejoice, weep with those who weep. ¹⁶ Live in harmony with one another. Do not be haughty, but associate with the lowly.[b] Never be wise in your own sight. ¹⁷ Repay no one evil for evil, but give thought to do what is honorable in the sight of all. 18 If possible, so far as it depends on you, live peaceably with all. ¹⁹ Beloved, never avenge yourselves, but leave it[c] to the wrath of God, for it is written, "Vengeance is mine, I will repay, says the Lord." ²⁰ To the contrary, "if your enemy is hungry, feed him; if he is thirsty, give him something to drink; for by so doing you will heap burning coals on his head." ²¹ Do not be overcome by evil, but overcome evil with good.

____

____

____

____

____

We are always to treat everybody with honor. The difficulty is with those who do not reciprocate and go further to hurt and oppose you, come against you, selfishly try to manipulate you, do things that are not just and fair knowing full well that they're not fair. He says, *When that occurs, as far as this is concerning you, make sure you are living in freedom and peace (shalom).*

What does that mean? God says that first this is just between you and Him. Is your heart in forgiveness—on the same basis that He has forgiven you? You deserve His wrath. You couldn't earn His forgiveness or opportunity for reconciliation and relationship because the requirement was perfection, and you cannot meet that. But, on His own nature He forgave you and removed the requirement to be perfect. You've got to get to this same place first. Have these people hurt you? Yes. Is what they did just? No. Do they deserve your anger? Yes. That's OK. But now that you understand that the first step is to go to forgiveness—which is just releasing the burden of the offense from your heart so that you don't carry it any further—you are then released from the burden and can live in freedom and peace (shalom).

Given that this concerns you now, make an effort to have those who oppose you come to peace about this as well. If He so directs, you can make an offer of reconciliation asking if they would be willing to process the truth with you. Sometimes God will give you the instruction not to even bother because He already knows the outcome. Maybe your offer is going to make things worse—not only are they going to reject it, but they're going to come against you harder and hurt you even further. Your offer only sets things backward and lessens any possibility of reconciliation.

God is talking about heart—as far as you are concerned, have you gone to forgiveness, and are you available in your heart to have Him direct you toward reconciliation or how to take the next step? Are you willing to take the next step with Him when they either reject your offer of reconciliation, or fail to process the truth and offend you? What about when God directs you not to even bother, what then?

What did David want to do that was supported by his men? He wanted to take vengeance. He wanted to establish the conclusion of this and make sure justice was served. There is often opportunity to do that, which is what happened with David when Saul was right in front of him. He had this opportunity, his men supported it and even interpreted it as God giving David the opportunity to take vengeance. God says not to look at the circumstances as if He's leading you to take vengeance. No, this is not of God. Vengeance is what? His. He will establish justice. He says to get out of the way so there is room for His wrath because His wrath is certain, and justice will be served. On what basis is God saying this?

> **Read Genesis 12:1–3:**
>
> The Call of Abram
>
> **12** Now the Lord said[a] to Abram, "Go from your country[b] and your kindred and your father's house to the land that I will show you. 2 And I will make of you a great nation, and I will bless you and make your name great, so that you will be a blessing. 3 I will bless those who bless you, and him who dishonors you I will curse, and in you all the families of the earth shall be blessed."[c]

____

____

____

____

____

God's Covenant is, *I will bless you to make you a blessing. I will bless those who bless you, and I will curse those who curse you.* Those who bless you are those who join you—meaning they're willing to process through to truth to get things worked out. You process until you get a solution—at least at the moment. David thought he and Saul had a solution—that Saul agreed to stop chasing him. Did he stop chasing him? No, which is why God told David to go into what's called the stronghold. The stronghold is His place of protection. Where was that? It was in the caves. *You have to keep living in the caves—but don't worry, vengeance is Mine,* said the Lord. David had to get out of the way so God could fulfill justice as this person is now cursed and will experience His wrath. Get out of the way, and don't enable them. Don't step in and rescue them. They're cursed. They are absolutely cursed. David could be released from this, which is why He didn't allow him to go deeper into the pain of what he was about to do—because then David would have been against Him, stepping into the place of cursing. Instead, David was to go to forgiveness and join Him in what He had already done—forgiven Saul and taken away the requirement to be perfect. It is now Saul's choice to either bless David or not, but if not, then he is cursed and will experience God's wrath. Since David was released from the burden of this, God will show him what to do next, which, in this case, was to forget it, dust off his feet, and move on. God will take care of it.

The truth of this was that Saul was still God's anointed until God made him no longer anointed in the role of king. This is independent of Saul's behavior. Even though Saul could have been the most evil person on the planet, he is God's anointed by the very position that God put him there. David needed to honor that since God had not put David in that position yet. God would guide David into freedom and his assignments, but he could also be assured that Saul was cursed, and justice will be served—by Him and not by David.

This also states that we are to bless those who persecute us—which seems contradictory to what we just learned. God says, *Get out of the way because this person is cursed, and I'm going to serve justice. Things are not going to go well for this person. I'm going to make sure that this person will experience consequences if they are not willing to process truth with you and resolve the offense.*

How would you bless somebody who is cursed, especially since God asked you to get out of the way and let His cursing be fulfilled? What is the only way that anyone can reverse God's curse? Remember, all stand condemned as people born with a sin nature, and cannot meet the requirement of perfection, and thus stand cursed—eternally separated from God. The only solution is repentance—to reverse any curse because of separation from God, once must repent. They must join Him by having the same heart. You can bless a person who is cursed by praying that the Father would work to invite them to repent. If and when they do, they immediately move from being cursed to blessed—since God has forgiven them and welcomes them—and all—back upon repentance. Our prayer continues to be that they would repent. We are not to take vengeance but know that God will until they repent, but then, upon them repenting, we rejoice and are actually excited that they then will be blessed and no longer cursed.

While in the position of being cursed, their situations are going to get worse, their life will be a mess, with awful circumstances. They are going to have things to overcome, so we pray that they wake up one day and are sorry that they haven't been willing to follow God or to work toward making things right with you. Once they repent, what happens? The curse is reversed, and they enter into the blessings of God overcoming—and all their problems will be resolved, especially the ones caused by not following God. You then rejoice because you get to see them live the life that is available to all of us.

God says that this process is really simple. They've hurt you. They deserve your anger. He knows this and agrees that they deserve your anger—but He has already forgiven them. When? At the cross. Now and forever, and it's true now. He's forgiven them, so join Him in that truth. You can forgive them, too, on the same basis that He forgave you, and then you can be free of that burden.

Because they are forgiven, does this also mean they are reconciled to God? No. Why? They have offended you and are still coming against you. You are His anointed, and you're walking with Him. Since they're coming against you, by definition, they are not reconciled to Him. Why then would you step in between that and attempt to force reconciliation by either caving to them or trying to take vengeance on your own? Rather, pray for repentance so that they can cross over from cursing—where it is absolute and vengeance is His—to blessing. He invites us to join Him with the same heart—living in freedom, letting go, knowing that justice will be served, and desiring blessing. When someone comes against us, are we to seek vengeance and make sure justice is served? Never. We don't have that right.

As we are seeking God to provide overcoming and deliverance through prayer, what does God remind us, and what does He call us to receive and live out? Why is this so important to Him overcoming, and what is the primary benefit to us?

Read Mark 11:20–25:

The Lesson from the Withered Fig Tree

[20] As they passed by in the morning, they saw the fig tree withered away to its roots. [21] And Peter remembered and said to him, "Rabbi, look! The fig tree that you cursed has withered." [22] And Jesus answered them, "Have faith in God. [23] Truly, I say to you, whoever says to this mountain, 'Be taken up and thrown into the sea,' and does not doubt in his heart, but believes that what he says will come to pass, it will be done for him. [24] Therefore I tell you, whatever you ask in prayer, believe that you have received[a] it, and it will be yours. [25] And whenever you stand praying, forgive, if you have anything against anyone, so that your Father also who is in heaven may forgive you your trespasses."[b]

____

____

____

____

LESSON 2:
WHAT ARE THE DIFFERENT ELEMENTS OF GOD PROVIDING OVERCOMING AND DELIVERANCE?

He says that when you are praying and learning how to hear His promises, His instructions, His path for fulfilling your prayers—because we are seeking and receiving His will—and I remind you that you have unforgiveness in your heart, what are you supposed to do? Stop. Why? You're holding a grudge. You're not representing Him, and that's not His heart. He has already forgiven them, but you have not joined Him in His heart toward them. So, before you proceed in praying to seek and receive His will, He is asking you to stop and pursue receiving and then experiencing forgiveness toward that person who has offended. This is critical. Why? Because, by definition, you're living back in the world and not in the Kingdom of God—as His nature is forgiveness and His nature is not operating in you.

He has not asked you to reconcile. That's up to you and the person who has offended you. But do have a heart to process with this person by going to truth. Do not cave, doing whatever they want to do, and do not seek vengeance on your own or hold a grudge. If you have forgiveness, you can get that resolved. Then you can go back to praying, and He will fulfill His will as you receive it and believe it. But if you don't go to forgiveness and live in His nature, you're stopped. David understood this, even when he was thinking the opposite. How did that happen? He went to truth and was led by whom? The Holy Spirit. David said, *Let God judge between you and me.* The Spirit confirmed this, and David knew that he was not supposed to take vengeance. Can you release it? Yes. David was living that out by being led by the Holy Spirit.

As we conclude this lesson, we've learned a couple of really important things about overcoming and deliverance. Make sure you have other spiritual followers of Christ in your life—spouse, friend, inner circle, small group—so that you do not go to discouragement and try to figure things out on your own. You need each other. The body is for that purpose—to together have a heart to go with Him, to seek Him and His will, and then make your decisions by checking in and asking, *Now what? What's Your will—which is best and none better?* When others offend you and come against you—go to forgiveness, be willing to reconcile, and process the truth versus caving or seeking revenge on your own. Rather, God says: *Let Me do it. Vengeance is Mine. You go to forgiveness. Let Me deal with it, and then move on. You will be free of the heaviness and burden and can move on into the beautiful things of life.*

"God is the One who overcomes and delivers."

As we continue with our course, *Overcoming and Deliverance: A Study of the Life of David*, we have do so by understanding some important things:

1. God is the One who overcomes and delivers.

2. In the world, you're going to have a need for this—but He can do it because He's preeminent, He has the power to do it, and He has the heart to do it. He promises that He is going to bless you to make you a blessing as He has come to overcome and to deliver, which He revealed in Isaiah 61.

3. He said the key is that we must have a heart to follow after Him, to follow His will.

4. We learned with David that when he came against opposition with Goliath, he responded with, *How dare he come against the living God? I know the truth of what God speaks, and so I'm willing to go into battle and come at him in the name of the Lord.*

5. David became discouraged when he wasn't appointed king on his timeline. He was lonely and all by himself. God says one of the important pieces of our life as believers is the body—fellowship with your spouse, your friends, your inner circle, you small group. Make sure that you're in fellowship with others who can come around you and assist you in what? Seeking God's will and providing confirmation of that will.

6. As David made decisions, he always checked in with God to see what the next step should be and how he should move forward. *I understand why we're here, but now what?*

7. When you have opposition, it is difficult to overcome the anger that you're dealing with as well as the fear and the anxiety caused by trying to figure out how to deal with people or situations that are coming against you. God says, *Vengeance is mine. You stay in freedom, go to forgiveness. Let Me heal you, let Me give you answers—I'll take care of it. Justice will be served, and I'm going to show you how to release it by moving on from it. If you can't move on from it, I'll teach you how to have boundaries.* David understood that because he went to the truth.

David has already learned some pretty amazing truths. He's learned that God will resolve issues. He's learned decision making and how to check in. He's learned forgiveness, and that God will give him answers. But now he comes into a new situation. We will learn why these lessons are so critical when, in a sense, David ignores all of that as we go to this next story.

Though David had learned that "Vengeance is Mine, sayeth the Lord," what happened in this situation that he responded differently? What caused him to respond this way? What did God do for David in this situation? Why? What was the benefit to David?

Read 1 Samuel 25:2–44:

2 And there was a man in Maon whose business was in Carmel. The man was very rich; he had three thousand sheep and a thousand goats. He was shearing his sheep in Carmel. 3 Now the name of the man was Nabal, and the name of his wife Abigail. The woman was discerning and beautiful, but the man was harsh and badly behaved; he was a Calebite. 4 David heard in the wilderness that Nabal was shearing his sheep. 5 So David sent ten young men. And David said to the young men, "Go up to Carmel, and go to Nabal and greet him in my name. 6 And thus you shall greet him: 'Peace be to you, and peace be to your house, and peace be to all that you have. 7 I hear that you have shearers. Now your shepherds have been with us, and we did them no harm, and they missed nothing all the time they were in Carmel. 8 Ask your young men, and they will tell you. Therefore let my young men find favor in your eyes, for we come on a feast day. Please give whatever you have at hand to your servants and to your son David.'"

9 When David's young men came, they said all this to Nabal in the name of David, and then they waited. 10 And Nabal answered David's servants, "Who is David? Who is the son of Jesse? There are many servants these days who are breaking away from their masters. 11 Shall I take my bread and my water and my meat that I have killed for my shearers and give it to men who come from I do not know where?" 12 So David's young men turned away and came back and told him all this. 13 And David said to his men, "Every man strap on his sword!" And every man of them strapped on his sword. David also strapped on his sword. And about four hundred men went up after David, while two hundred remained with the baggage.

14 But one of the young men told Abigail, Nabal's wife, "Behold, David sent messengers out of the wilderness to greet our master, and he railed at them. 15 Yet the men were very good to us, and we suffered no harm, and we did not miss anything when we were in the fields, as long as we went with them. 16 They were a wall to us both by night and by day, all the while we were with them keeping the sheep. 17 Now therefore know this and consider what you should do, for harm is determined against our master and against all his house, and he is such a worthless man that one cannot speak to him."

18 Then Abigail made haste and took two hundred loaves and two skins of wine and five sheep already prepared and five seahs[a] of parched grain and a hundred clusters of raisins and two hundred cakes of figs, and laid them on donkeys. 19 And she said to her young men, "Go on before me; behold, I come after you." But she did not tell her husband Nabal. 20 And as she rode on the donkey and came down under cover of the mountain, behold, David and his men came down toward her, and she met them. 21 Now David had said, "Surely in vain have I guarded all that this fellow has in the wilderness, so that nothing was missed of all that belonged to him, and he has returned me evil for good. 22 God do so to the enemies of David[b] and more also, if by morning I leave so much as one male of all who belong to him."

23 When Abigail saw David, she hurried and got down from the donkey and fell before David on her face and bowed to the ground. 24 She fell at his feet and said, "On me alone, my lord, be the guilt. Please let your servant speak in your ears, and hear the words of your servant. 25 Let not my lord regard this worthless fellow, Nabal, for as his name is, so is he. Nabal[c] is his name, and folly is with him. But I your servant did not see the young men of my lord, whom you sent. 26 Now then, my lord, as the Lord lives, and as your soul lives,

because the Lord has restrained you from bloodguilt and from saving with your own hand, now then let your enemies and those who seek to do evil to my lord be as Nabal. [27] And now let this present that your servant has brought to my lord be given to the young men who follow my lord. [28] Please forgive the trespass of your servant. For the Lord will certainly make my lord a sure house, because my lord is fighting the battles of the Lord, and evil shall not be found in you so long as you live. [29] If men rise up to pursue you and to seek your life, the life of my lord shall be bound in the bundle of the living in the care of the Lord your God. And the lives of your enemies he shall sling out as from the hollow of a sling. [30] And when the Lord has done to my lord according to all the good that he has spoken concerning you and has appointed you prince[d] over Israel, [31] my lord shall have no cause of grief or pangs of conscience for having shed blood without cause or for my lord working salvation himself. And when the Lord has dealt well with my lord, then remember your servant."

[32] And David said to Abigail, "Blessed be the Lord, the God of Israel, who sent you this day to meet me! [33] Blessed be your discretion, and blessed be you, who have kept me this day from bloodguilt and from working salvation with my own hand! [34] For as surely as the Lord, the God of Israel, lives, who has restrained me from hurting you, unless you had hurried and come to meet me, truly by morning there had not been left to Nabal so much as one male." [35] Then David received from her hand what she had brought him. And he said to her, "Go up in peace to your house. See, I have obeyed your voice, and I have granted your petition."

[36] And Abigail came to Nabal, and behold, he was holding a feast in his house, like the feast of a king. And Nabal's heart was merry within him, for he was very drunk. So she told him nothing at all until the morning light. [37] In the morning, when the wine had gone out of Nabal, his wife told him these things, and his heart died within him, and he became as a stone. [38] And about ten days later the Lord struck Nabal, and he died.

[39] When David heard that Nabal was dead, he said, "Blessed be the Lord who has avenged the insult I received at the hand of Nabal, and has kept back his servant from wrongdoing. The Lord has returned the evil of Nabal on his own head." Then David sent and spoke to Abigail, to take her as his wife. [40] When the servants of David came to Abigail at Carmel, they said to her, "David has sent us to you to take you to him as his wife." [41] And she rose and bowed with her face to the ground and said, "Behold, your handmaid is a servant to wash the feet of the

servants of my lord." [42] And Abigail hurried and rose and mounted a donkey, and her five young women attended her. She followed the messengers of David and became his wife.

[43] David also took Ahinoam of Jezreel, and both of them became his wives. [44] Saul had given Michal his daughter, David's wife, to Palti the son of Laish, who was of Gallim.

____

____

____

____

____

This is a story that reveals the deeper process of overcoming and deliverance as we continue to learn and walk in truth. Prior to this, David had gone through the situation with Saul and the opportunity to take justice into his own hands. The Holy Spirit checked him and revealed the heart and will of God when someone is unjust, hurting you, and opposing you. Vengeance is His. You go to forgiveness, and He will take care of it. He had just learned this through the situations at Keilah, but now what? He's learned much and is living out these truths.

David again finds himself in the wilderness, hiding in caves, and comes across servants of a noble man, who are taking care of sheep. Because of his prior experience with taking care of sheep, he knows all about this and vows to protect them. He understand how they work and what they need, and he says he will protect them, which he does. When it comes time for the festival feast of shearing, where they will be having a big party with lots of food, gaiety, and games, David believes that if he sends a few of his men to tell them what he has done, they would be pleased to give them some of the extra food that they will not miss. They were sick of living in caves, chasing down food for themselves, all the while Nabal was having this big feast that they made possible by protecting his servants. Of course, Nabal would give them the extra food.

What happens instead? Nabal says, *No way, I'm not doing this. Who are you? I'm not giving you anything.* When David's men came back and told him that Nabal refused to give them anything, David said, *That's it. We're going after them, and we're going to kill every single one of them. Their wives, their children, their livestock. We're going to kill everything. Let's go.* And they go.

After all that David had learned, why would he respond this way? He knew that vengeance belonged to the Lord and that justice would be served by the Lord. David was supposed to let it go, release his anger through forgiveness, and move on. But how did he respond? He let his anger get the best of them. He went straight to anger, and his anger just took over. He was not going to put up with this and was going to go take care of this on his own. Off he went with his men in tow and now: *Vengeance is mine*, sayeth David. *I am going to serve justice.*

What happens? Abigail shows up with food and says, *Hold on just a second. I understand what you're doing, and I understand why you're doing it*—even though she didn't. But she continues, asking David if he really wanted to do this and violate what God has shown him. She explains how he was going to fail because if he was going to take his own vengeance then have God would come against him. She tells him that he should reconsider. David, having heard it, what does he do? He agrees.

Abigail is described as a woman who has a discerning heart. The Holy Spirit views her as a willing vessel, who knows and sees the truth clearly, with a heart to then speak to David this truth as a messenger of God. She is well informed. *David, you've been anointed king. You're going to become the king. The Holy Spirit has shown me that what you're about to do is going to disqualify you. Are you sure you want to violate God's will? This isn't of God. I can't confirm that what you're about to do is God's will. I would suggest you reconsider, David.*

David thanks her for being the messenger of God—as he knows that it was God who prevented him from doing this. How did God prevent him? He sent a person. Did the Holy Spirit make an attempt? Yes. David ignored it completely. Because his button had been pushed, he had no ability to hear the voice of the Spirit. Then God sends a person. *I'm representing God, I'm telling you that you ought to reconsider. I can't confirm that what you're doing is God's will. You need to reconsider.* And that point, David received the message loud and clear. He understood and told his men they were going back. They were not going to do this because God had already helped him, and they understood vengeance belonged to whom? God. It was not David's, and it was not theirs—even in this scenario, when Nabal deserved the justice they wanted to serve.

God will take care of serving justice. *Do not fail at following what you already know to be true—as it gives you freedom and release from the burdens that you might carry—those burdens that were about to become severe consequences—not for Nabal, but for you. Though you did not respond to My prompting as you did with Saul, I sent another messenger who intervened—and you were willing to hear her voice, and knew that was from Me.*

David got to see God's vengeance when God killed Nabal only 10 days later. This is an example of God working with so many different people and scenarios and knitting it all together with Abigail serving as the central character to fulfill God's purpose.

As you're seeking God's will and you want to overcome, sometimes your buttons are going to be pushed, sometimes the opposition will just get to you. You are upset. Things happen, maybe it's an audit from the IRS or a major roadblock at work, or difficulty in your family. Whatever it is, it gets under your skin, and before you even realize it, you are trying to take care of the situation on your own. Just like in David's situation, God will send somebody. You may not be following the Holy Spirit at all, but God still cares about you and will keep trying to get you to make the right choice. So, He'll send somebody who will say, *I cannot confirm that what you are doing is of God—I suggest you reconsider*. When you hear that, what is God speaking to you? You need to stop and reconsider. Follow Him to His way, His will, His best for you. When God sends Abigail, pay attention, and follow.

In the following situation, in what way did Peter respond to what Jesus said was going to happen? What did Jesus say to him? What was the reason? As we are seeking to follow God, what then did Jesus say are the steps to following Him? What do these mean, and how are we then to live daily?

Read Matthew 16:20–25:

20 Then he strictly charged the disciples to tell no one that he was the Christ.

Jesus Foretells His Death and Resurrection
21 From that time Jesus began to show his disciples that he must go to Jerusalem and suffer many things from the elders and chief priests and scribes, and be killed, and on the third day be raised. 22 And Peter took him aside and began to rebuke him, saying, "Far be it from you, Lord![a] This shall never happen to you." 23 But he turned and said to Peter, "Get behind me, Satan! You are a hindrance[b] to me. For you are not setting your mind on the things of God, but on the things of man."

Take Up Your Cross and Follow Jesus
24 Then Jesus told his disciples, "If anyone would come after me, let him deny himself and take up his cross and follow me. 25 For whoever would save his life[c] will lose it, but whoever loses his life for my sake will find it.

____

____

____

____

____

Peter listened as Christ spoke of His impending suffering, His death, and also His resurrection. Peter responded that he would never let that happen. If we asked Peter to look at what he was about to do, what would his viewpoint be? He would say that it was a good thing, a noble idea, and the right thing to do—to protect his Messiah. Jesus looks at him and says, *Get behind Me, Satan. You're about to do the opposite of My will. You think it's a good idea, but this is not My will. Get behind Me, Satan.*

Why does Jesus respond this way? Because He says, *You don't have the things of God, you have the things of men on your mind—what you've decided.* Peter said that he was intending to act according to what he thought was a good idea—just as David did when he was acting out of his anger and his own distorted heart.

This is really simple. Why didn't Peter have the things of God on his heart? He forgot a step—he didn't ask Christ what he should do. Jesus was telling His disciples about how He would suffer, die, and be resurrected. They had no idea what He was talking about, and it didn't make sense to them. They thought He was the Messiah and that He was going to rule. What was Jesus talking about? If Peter would have asked Jesus to explain it to him, he would have been pursuing the things of God. But instead, Peter decided, based upon what he had heard, that he was going to do what he thought was best. Why? He forgot the check in.

What did David forget when he rallied his troops to go kill Nabal? He forgot to check in and consider what was on the heart of God. *God, what would You have me do?* God would have said, *David, I thought you and I had this settled already. Vengeance is Mine. I'll take care of it. Don't worry about this. I got this.* It would have saved him all the hassle and difficulty of moving to act out of anger and vengeance. He was going to go kill everybody. Fortunately, God sends Abigail. What is the key to how we are to follow God? We are to deny self. Take up the cross and follow Him.

Why would you follow Him? Because you surrendered your will to Him. You are willing to follow His will. So, when you are checked by an "Abigail," God is saying, *I'm trying to show you something—this is not awful—its Hallelujah.* He's going to show you something that's important for you to join His will. Don't become Satan and say you don't care—which in a sense is what David had done. He didn't care. He wanted to take vengeance. He was about to make a huge mistake when he strayed from following God. When David realized through the intervention of Abigail that he was not following God, he again denied self, took up the cross, and followed Him.

As we are following Him, what can we learn from how David? He prayed for clarity and understanding of what God was revealing to him. What truths are to be received so that we can be assured that this revelation will be fulfilled? Why is this important? What then is the expectation of God's promise to overcome and deliver us?

Read 2 Samuel 7:25–29:

25 And now, O Lord God, confirm forever the word that you have spoken concerning your servant and concerning his house, and do as you have spoken. 26 And your name will be magnified forever, saying, 'The Lord of hosts is God over Israel,' and the house of your servant David will be established before you. 27 For you, O Lord of hosts, the God of Israel, have made this revelation to your servant, saying, 'I will build you a house.' Therefore your servant has found courage to pray this prayer to you. 28 And now, O Lord God, you are God, and your words are true, and you have promised this good thing to your servant. 29 Now therefore may it please you to bless the house of your servant, so that it may continue forever before you. For you, O Lord God, have spoken, and with your blessing shall the house of your servant be blessed forever."

____

____

____

____

____

The context here is that David had decided it would be good idea for him to build God a temple—because they have been moving around the Tabernacle from place to place to place. He wanted to build Him a permanent temple. He goes to Nathan, who was a prophet, to seek confirmation. Nathan agrees that it is a great idea and tells David to go ahead and do it. God then tells Nathan that when David came to get confirmation from him, he forgot something important. Nathan failed to check in with Him. Had he checked in with God, he would have known that David should not be building a temple for God. The answer was no, absolutely not. *David is a man of war. He cannot build it. His son will build Me a temple, but not him.* What Nathan confirmed came out of his own flesh. He forgot this very important step in following God—to check in with Him. God says to Nathan, *You didn't ask Me, and so you are not following Me, but I am going to reveal My will to you for David. Tell David that My promise is that his lineage is going to produce the Messiah, who's going to save all of mankind. As you follow Me and you have a heart to follow Me, your lineage will produce the Messiah—this is My Word, My promise, My will for you.*

David received what God had to say, and says to God, *I found courage in my heart to pray to You.* What was David praying? *What does this promise mean, and what does it mean for me? Help me understand this. It is not clear to me.* His prayer was a dialogue. *What are You saying? God, what's Your promise to me? What is Your will? I need to process that.* He had found courage—the strength to pursue a dialogue with God to understand and receive what God was fully speaking and going to fulfill. He had courage in the heart to be willing to go get the answer—to get clarity. He continued until he received this clarity on three important things:

1. He is God, and David is not. David is saying what? *God, You are capable, fully able to fulfill what You just said. You are God, You are the Almighty. Nothing is superior to You. You can do this, and I believe it.*

2. His words (equivalent to the Greek word—Rhema) that He had spoken to David are true. Absolutely true—no doubt at all. This is going to happen. David understood His will.

3. These words, these promises were applicable to David personally, to his situation and particularly as they were looking at overcoming.

We, too, can find courage in our heart to seek God's Word, His promise to us—the courage to ask Him what He has to say about problems that we might have. Then we can see how He applies this truth to us personally and are given confirmation.

Courage is having a heart to process through with God to believing prayer. Do you understand His will? Is it clear to you? Do you believe it? When you get to faith—belief, you can speak verse 29, *Amen. So be it—may it please You to now fulfill what You just said. Now that I have these three understandings and I believe them, I expect You to complete it—may it be so, may it please you to make it so.*

As we pursue God's will, we will have lots of questions. How are we to seek answers to these questions? What does God promise as we ask? Why is this so important to our seeking God's will?

> **Read 1 Kings 10:1–3:**
>
> The Queen of Sheba
> **10** Now when the queen of Sheba heard of the fame of Solomon concerning the name of the LORD, she came to test him with hard questions. [2] She came to Jerusalem with a very great retinue, with camels bearing spices and very much gold and precious stones. And when she came to Solomon, she told him all that was on her mind. [3] And Solomon answered all her questions; there was nothing hidden from the king that he could not explain to her.

The Queen of Sheba came to Solomon seeking wisdom—which took humility on her part—acknowledging that even though she was a "big shot," a queen, and supposed to be a wise leader, she realized that she needed more wisdom and went to the one who had demonstrated his wisdom. This is our requirement as well—to understand that we do not have the answers—that we need wisdom, and in humility, we are to go to God to receive wisdom. What did the Queen of Sheba ask Solomon? She asked him every hard question she had.

What are your hard questions? You've got a problem—a real problem, something in your life has happened—a negative circumstance, adversity. Things are not working as you hoped. You need to know what you should do and what God has to say about your situation. So, you go to God with all your hard questions—addiction, problems with anger, fear, anxiety, and patterns in your life that you are struggling with. You ask God how He is going to handle these issues and what's going to happen. You need answers and resolution.

Solomon, who was representing God, did what? He answered every single question. God says, *I got this. There is nothing that I won't give you. Nothing is too difficult for Me. Why? Because I know it—absolutely; and I can make it happen. Your circumstances are subordinate to My spiritual power, My Word, My authority.*

To discern God's will, what is the process of using our inner circle to hear, receive, and then believe what God's will is? Why is this such a privilege for us to be able to discover His will?

Read Matthew 18:18–20:

[18] Truly, I say to you, whatever you bind on earth shall be bound in heaven, and whatever you loose on earth shall be loosed[a] in heaven. [19] Again I say to you, if two of you agree on earth about anything they ask, it will be done for them by my Father in heaven. [20] For where two or three are gathered in my name, there am I among them."

____

____

____

____

____

As you are gathering with your inner circle (spouse, friend, small group, etc.), you are pursuing answers from God about hard questions. You have a problem, a decision, a difficult circumstance, a big relationship conflict—and you need answers. God says, *Go with your inner circle and pray "in My name."* What are you praying for? God's will—His promise, His word as it applies to you, and each of us personally. You ask God what He has to say about all this. He also says that with your inner circle, work together to come to unity. Who are you to come to unity with? The Spirit. You are to make every effort to go to unity with the Spirit, so that you can pray as David did. You now know to find courage in your heart to process until you understand these things about the Father:

1. You are God.

2. What you've said is true.

3. You've applied this to us personally.

We got it. We understand, have clarity, are now in unity with the Spirit, and we have discovered Your will. It is then we can pray, *Amen, so be it—may it please You to do it.* Think about where most of your time is to be spent as you're gathering to pray together—to receive His will. That takes time. That takes processing, that takes dialogue and asking, seeking, and knocking. You might need some more information or help understanding what it is all about. What's His promise? That's where our energy goes. That's where the time goes—which is opposed to just praying what we want God to do for us—*God, I have a problem, take care of it, and let me know when You do.* That's how we tend to pray. It's a wish, not much happens, and we get discouraged, thinking God's must have said no. God says, *You never asked Me about My will, you never spent the energy to find courage in your heart, you never got to unity with the Spirit, and you never received confirmation that you know My will.* When you do, guess what is going to happen? You get to the same place that David did and get to experience the fulfillment of God's will. You have the power of binding and loosing—loosing the power of heaven into this situation and binding off the enemy that is coming against you to attempt to thwart God's will for you.

Let's look at another situation with David—his personal failure. What was the situation that led to his problem? He's supposed to go to war but decides that he has been to war enough and is just going to stay home and send everybody else. He's out on his roof, basically doing nothing, and he sees who? Bathsheba, who's beautiful and naked.

Now, as a man, when you look at a beautiful woman and see that she is naked, it is automatically stimulating since men respond to physical attraction. As followers of God, we are supposed to acknowledge this but then go back to normal life without any further thought or pursuit. What did David do? He kept looking and decided that he wanted her. He tells his servant to go get her and bring her to him where he then commits adultery.

Then, what happens? Bathsheba gets pregnant. She's having David's baby. David knows this isn't good because her husband is at war, and they're going to ask her how it happened. David comes up with the scheme to have Uriah come back to lay with his wife. Uriah comes back, but tells David he can't lay with his wife, because everybody else is at war. He can't because he needs to get back to the war.

Spiraling even farther into his desperation, David comes up with this elaborate scheme to have his own army set up a situation that will result in Uriah being killed by the enemy. This works and Uriah is killed, murdered. As far as David is concerned, his plan worked fine, and he is functioning without guilt or remorse.

Read 2 Samuel 12:

Nathan Rebukes David

12 And the LORD sent Nathan to David. He came to him and said to him, "There were two men in a certain city, the one rich and the other poor. [2] The rich man had very many flocks and herds, [3] but the poor man had nothing but one little ewe lamb, which he had bought. And he brought it up, and it grew up with him and with his children. It used to eat of his morsel and drink from his cup and lie in his arms,[a] and it was like a daughter to him. [4] Now there came a traveler to the rich man, and he was unwilling to take one of his own flock or herd to prepare for the guest who had come to him, but he took the poor man's lamb and prepared it for the man who had come to him." [5] Then David's anger was greatly kindled against the man, and he said to Nathan, "As the LORD lives, the man who has done this deserves to die, [6] and he shall restore the lamb fourfold, because he did this thing, and because he had no pity."

> [7] Nathan said to David, "You are the man! Thus says the Lord, the God of Israel, 'I anointed you king over Israel, and I delivered you out of the hand of Saul. [8] And I gave you your master's house and your master's wives into your arms and gave you the house of Israel and of Judah. And if this were too little, I would add to you as much more. [9] Why have you despised the word of the LORD, to do what is evil in his sight? You have struck down Uriah the Hittite with the sword and have taken his wife to be your wife and have killed him with the sword of the Ammonites. [10] Now therefore the sword shall never depart from your house, because you have despised me and have taken the wife of Uriah the Hittite to be your wife.' [11] Thus says the Lord, 'Behold, I will raise up evil against you out of your own house. And I will take your wives before your eyes and give them to your neighbor, and he shall lie with your wives in the sight of this sun. [12] For you did it secretly, but I will do this thing before all Israel and before the sun.'" [13] David said to Nathan, "I have sinned against the LORD." And Nathan said to David, "The Lord also has put away your sin; you shall not die. [14] Nevertheless, because by this deed you have utterly scorned the LORD,[b] the child who is born to you shall die." [15] Then Nathan went to his house.

____

____

____

____

____

God sends Nathan, the prophet, to speak to David. He wants Nathan to tell David that He knows what is going on and to tell David this story to see how he responds. Nathan goes to David and tells him the story. David was furious against the man of the story, and said to Nathan, *As the Lord lives, a man who has done this shall surely die. He shall restore the lamb four-fold because he did this thing and had no pity.*

Nathan said to David, *You are the man. Thus, says the Lord God of Israel, "I delivered you king over Israel, I delivered you from the hand of Saul, I gave you your master's house and your master's wives into your keeping and gave you the House of Israel. If that had not been too little, I'd have given you even more. Why have you despised the truth—the will of the Lord, to do evil in My sight—you have killed Uriah the Hittite with the sword, you've taken his wife to be your wife. Therefore, the sword shall never depart from your house because you have despised Me and have taken his wife." Thus, says the Lord God. "Behold, I will raise up adversity against you from your own house, and I will take your wives before your eyes. You did it secretly, but I will do this thing before all Israel.*

David responds to Nathan, *This is all me. Yes, I have sinned*. Nathan tells David that today the Lord has put away his sin. David shall not die because of the deeds he had done. In other words, God forgave him. He has been forgiven. With this awful thing—murder and adultery, that's pretty high up on the list, but from God's perspective, the sin is not what David had done, but rather that he did all this in the self, he stopped walking with Him, and left the Kingdom.

Why and how did this all happen? What had David done to find himself in this position? He stopped abiding and separated himself from God and the life of God. So what happened to his mind? His mind went to selfishness—onto other things that were not the things of God—which is the default position for all of us. He had all these years of victory, of intimacy with God, of learning the great truths of God, of being delivered and having circumstances overcome, but when he stopped abiding, his default was immediately to go to the flesh—away from God, opposite of God. One might assume that after being anointed by the Holy Spirit, he would have realized that what he was doing was not right. He didn't even get to that point. He just accepted it as being something he deserved, and he justified it in the flesh. Upon hearing Nathan's story, he again received the truth of God and repented. He understood that he had sinned and repented from going to the flesh and sinning against God.

In Psalm 51, he goes into great explanation about how he was self-centered. He sinned, and his sins were not only against them—he also sinned against who? God. He prayed that God would give him back the joy of life and the joy of his salvation. And he also prayed that God would not take the Holy Spirit from him and to please let him return to that life. Repentance.

The Lord struck the child that David had with Bathsheba, and he became ill. David pleaded with God for the child, and he fasted and went in and lay all night on the ground. The elders of the house went to him to raise him up from the ground, but he would not. Nor did he eat food with them. On the seventh day, it came to pass that the child died. The servants of David were afraid to tell him that his child was dead because when the child was alive, they had spoken to him and he would not heed their voice. How can we tell him the child is dead? They were worried he might harm himself.

When David saw that his servants were whispering, he perceived that the child was dead and asked a servant if the child was dead. The servant confirmed this, and David rose, washed and anointed himself, changed his clothes, went to the House of the Lord, and worshipped. Then he went to his own house and requested they set food before him—and he ate. His servant asked him what he was doing since he fasted and wept for the child while he was alive, but now that he was dead, David was now eating. David said, *While the child was alive, I fasted to request that God would heal the child and let the child live, but now he is dead. Why should I fast? Can I bring him back again? I shall go to him, but he shall not return to me.* And then he went in and laid with Bathsheba and had Solomon. David moved on.

When you sin, God will present the truth to you, just as David was presented with the truth. Yes, you have sinned, but God's going to get you to that truth. If what you're doing isn't of Him, He will try to check you but if that doesn't work, remember that the Spirit could use another person to present this truth to you. You are the one causing this problem. You've got adversity because of your actions. You've done this. But immediately, He says the remedy is what? Repent and come on back, which David did, but his leaving the Kingdom did not come without a consequence. What David did caused a consequence. When he asked God to reverse the consequence, God said, *no.* So, David fasts and mourns, and through this asks God if it is possible that He would reverse the consequence? God doesn't, and the child dies.

As soon as the child dies, David moves forward with his life. He can't go back and change it. He knows that he is the cause of this, but he has been released from guilt because God released him. God has forgiven him, David then forgives himself, and he goes back to living his life. The servants are surprised that David isn't sad about what he did, what he caused. But David says he is not sad because he has been forgiven.

That's the beauty of overcoming. You've been in the flesh, trying to figure things out. You are trying so hard. But you have to repent and say what: *Therefore, now there is now no condemnation for those who are in Christ, Jesus for the Spirit of life has set you free* (Romans 8:1–2). In other words, get to the point where you're at the same place that God is—where you are fully forgiven, and remember that God doesn't have a hierarchy of sin. He doesn't measure sin making those who commit more serious offenses take longer to get to forgiveness. His forgiveness is done already—it was completed for the past, present, and future. God released us from the consequences of walking away from Him and living in the flesh—the self.

What did Paul learn that was significant to him following God? What does that mean to how we are to approach our lives? Why is this so important to our following God into His steps of overcoming and deliverance?

Read Philippians 3:12–16:

Straining Toward the Goal

[12] Not that I have already obtained this or am already perfect, but I press on to make it my own, because Christ Jesus has made me his own. [13] Brothers, I do not consider that I have made it my own. But one thing I do: forgetting what lies behind and straining forward to what lies ahead, [14] I press on toward the goal for the prize of the upward call of God in Christ Jesus. [15] Let those of us who are mature think this way, and if in anything you think otherwise, God will reveal that also to you. [16] Only let us hold true to what we have attained.

____

____

____

____

____

Paul says, he has learned one thing. He has actually learned a lot, but this one thing is pretty significant. He forgets the past for things that he has already done, they're moot. Whether they're problems or even successes, he is not going to stay living there, he's going to move on. Instead, it is always, *Now what?* When David was successful at Keilah, what did he say? He forgot what just happened, but now what? When he just had this great sin and great consequence, he says, he can forget that and do what? Move on to the next part of his life.

This is something that really has to sink in. If you are going to have Him overcome, He can't afford for you to be thinking backwards. The past doesn't matter. He can take care of this now that you have repented and returned to being with Him. David, even in his extreme failure, understood that yes, it would have been better if he hadn't done any of that. Interesting enough, Solomon wouldn't have been born. Another son would have been born from David's other wife, and he would have been the builder of the temple. That was God's will. David altered that will. And what did God then say? He's got it from here. He's got a new plan. From here, He can fulfill what he is about to do. What do you have to do? Forget the things that lay behind and press on to the high calling of Christ Jesus.

As we approach our difficult circumstances for which we need overcoming and deliverance, what does God promise? What does that mean for our expecting victory? Why?

Read Psalm 34:8–12:

8 Oh, taste and see that the Lord is good!
  Blessed is the man who takes refuge in him!
9 Oh, fear the Lord, you his saints,
  for those who fear him have no lack!
10 The young lions suffer want and hunger;
  but those who seek the Lord lack no good thing.
11 Come, O children, listen to me;
  I will teach you the fear of the Lord.
12 What man is there who desires life
  and loves many days, that he may see good?

God will deliver you from what? All of your trouble—your broken-heartedness. He'll restore that. Not anything good is going to be withheld from you. God can do it. God's going to do it. If it involves people who are opposing me, He will take care of that, too. Who's the overcomer? God. God will overcome. Is it only certain difficulties, certain types of trouble? No, it's all. What about the really hard ones? Absolutely. Nothing's impossible with Him. Nothing. So therefore, all will be taken care of—all.

As you look at overcoming and deliverance, let's summarize what we have learned. Do you need it? Yes. When? All the time, because in the world, we're going to have trouble. This is the nature of the world, and we are not exempt. He will not solve all of this for the world, and He will not eliminate evil. God says, *No, you handed the authority over to Satan. He's got it. I've got to take it back through you. At the end, it'll be fully taken care of, but not until then. You're living in a wicked place, and you're going to have trouble. So, stop asking Me to solve all evil in the world. Rather, you are going to experience this trouble so the better thing to ask Me would be what? What do You have to say about this problem?*

God has given us the Covenant and is going to bless us to make us a blessing. He is going to bless those who bless us and curse those who curse us. He said he is going to restore to us so that we can live this grand life with Him. David fully understood that God will take care of all his issues, including his own ridiculous mistake. Yet, we still think, *How could David, who was a man after God's own heart and desired to do all God's will, do that?* He stopped abiding. No one is exempt from experiencing the consequences of severing the relationship with God.

That's why the life of abiding is so critical. Are you going to have trouble? Yes. Do you need things to be overcome circumstantially? Yes. Do you have issues of your heart that fall into patterns? Yes. What does He say? He will take care of all of them. Let's have a heart to go, even when we've gone to the flesh and walked away from God. Forget the things that lay behind and press onto the high calling of Christ Jesus.

Move on from concentrating on the problem and getting discouraged to knowing that this circumstance, this heart wound will be resolved and restored. Like David, surround yourself with people who will come alongside you to seek God's will together. He will give to you—His will. He'll overcome both circumstances and issues of your heart—and you can begin living this grand life that He has planned for you. He will bless you to become a blessing.